SPEDS
(Special Education Students)

An inside view and experiences
of educational systems by a Sped

Mirian Detres-Hickey PhD

authorHOUSE®

AuthorHouse™ LLC
1663 Liberty Drive
Bloomington, IN 47403
www.authorhouse.com
Phone: 1-800-839-8640

Published by AuthorHouse   07/08/2014

ISBN: 978-1-4969-2143-7 (sc)
ISBN: 978-1-4969-2144-4 (hc)
ISBN: 978-1-4969-2142-0 (e)

Dedication

This book is dedicated to the all the wonderful Speds I worked with throughout my 37+ years in Special Education. They taught me to be the passionate teacher and administrator that I am today. They were truly special and I thank God that I was able to have so many experiences that shaped my life.

I also dedicate this book to the wonderful late Howard Brodsky may he rest in peace and Pete Perlow who had faith in my madness and taught me how to be a better teacher. They knew that I was there to help and care for these kids. Lastly, thank you to my kids David, Danny, Bobby, Jennifer, and Kryssy who had to share me with so many other children. My children never complained. We should all understand disabilities and the need for respect and caring simply because we are all disabled in someway.

Thank you, and Love you all
Mirian

Contents

VI. Southern Sped School

VII. Mid-Western State Alternate High School

VIII. Are These Reasonable Accommodation Request Hmmmmmmm

IX. Terms you may need to know

Introduction

Let me introduce myself to you. My name is Mirian Detres, although I have a PhD, and two Master degrees, and I am also a Sociology Professor, I am first and foremost a SPED. A Sped is a special person that has a disability. I have multiple disabilities. However, most people that know me, don't know that. I am acutely Dyslexic, I have a profound hearing loss in my right ear and due to an illness I got in my older years, I lost quite a bit of sight in my right eye as well. So, instead of saying all of that, I just say I'm a SPED. I use the term "SPED" throughout the book. Most Special Education Teachers know the term. It is a term that is not known by the general public until now. I'm going to change that right now.

I think the public deserves to known what is only known by students and teachers of the special education system. With the understanding that you do not use it unless you are a sped yourself. It's like slang names, it's not cruel; it's an endearment, like sweetie, darling, etc. Or knuckle head. you use them among each other but don't let any other/ outsider use it, it would be very offensive. With that understood, "SPED", is a combination of the words "Special Education", which identifies those students that have a disability and are in special education classes.

I never wanted to be a teacher nor did I want kids. Both of which, I negated on. I became a mother of 6 children and a teacher of hundreds of students throughout the 30+ years; all of which were Speds. We are a special breed. We don't think as others do. Yet they don't seem to realize it. They continue to expect us to act like them and do the same things they do. We wear white clothes and summer garment's in the

1

rain and the winter, and we wear wool in the summer. As I said, we just don't think the same way as the rest of the population. Remember, we are always trying to compensate. Not compete, but compensate very different. Not just in life but in trying to live life. I tend to joke a lot, or should I say I use to. Hey, after 60 you tend to lose your sense of humor.

I haven't taught special education in 10 years. I've been in higher education teaching and in administration. However, I was a Special Education teacher, grades k – 12 and a testing assessor for 20+ years. I taught in New York City 600 schools, (those were schools for the behaviorally challenged) I taught in Florida schools, (which were horrible) I taught in Texas, (they have good structure but are crazy) and in Long Island. I spent most of my teaching years in Long Island.

I decided to become an administrator after years of seeing the difficulty new teacher were having in getting acclimated to a school district and specially to the students, I decided I wanted to teach the new bee's in teaching so they understand what they will be faced with. I wanted to have a major impact in the new teachers that were coming into the field that knew nothing and only had the book smarts and the false competency of student teaching as to knowing what makes these special individuals tick. Each year we had new regulations, policies, and labels for our special needs students. No wonder they were confused.

You should know I have taught the gamete of types of special needs individuals from the 3 years of age autistic children, which after crapping would play with their feces then rub it on my clothes; to working with the Alternate heavy duty teens that were emotionally disabled students. This population tried to beat me and to shoot me.

One actually did shot at me. I have taught from the K grade to high school and now college level special needs students. I have taught the Learning Disabled on all grades and most of the other disabilities. I conducted assessment testing for years in Spanish for two school districts on Long Island, and in New York City. Another bit of news you need to be aware of if you are planning on going into teaching, you have to have a sense of humor, be a little crazy, but have control and purpose over that craziness. If you don't then my friend you would be lost and they will eat you alive.

But I'd be lying if I told you that I didn't like teaching the Emotionally Disabled (ED) the most. I have a spot in my heart for them. They are the most creative, entertaining and usually the brightest youngsters that you have ever dealt with. They don't pull punches. If these kids don't like someone, there is a reason and you better listen to them. Unfortunately, many have their parents involved in 97% of their lives and therefore, they cannot develop nor express themselves fully as adults. I guess I was fortunate that my folks didn't care too much about me so I developed and learned responsibility. Something many students that have controlling parents don't get a chance to do.

Anyway, these are stories that happened to me as a Sped Teacher in three different states. By the way, I discovered as crowed and full of complaints as the New York School Districts have, they are by far the better educational system compared to the ones I experienced working in.

Another thing you should be aware of, is when a Sped tells you they don't care, take their word for it, they do not care. So, trying to threaten them on any level to do something, they would probably want you to try something. They just don't see the consequences that come later. Their life is of now for the moment. I'm not saying all of them are this way, but a good majority of them are, with me included.

So, with this said, if I have a choice of what population of students to work with, I would have to say without a doubt, the emotionally disabled pop. Not only are they out there, but they can keep you laughing!

I realized in my earlier teaching years children no matter what age need two things in order to grow and learn. That is to be treated individually according to their needs and to be trusted and cared for. I loved my students and still do. It was Christmas every September for me. I was like a child, wanting to see my new children. I was at the school setting up my plans and room a few weeks prior to the beginning of school every year. It was and still is so exciting for me when September comes along. When the first day of class begun. The new students were like clumps of clay or a canvas and I was the artist. I had the major responsibility of molding them or helping create something beautiful and give them something they can always recall and reflect in life.

I felt I had to help them learn to succeed in life no matter what disability they had. Those students became my children for the year. It didn't matter their age. I always felt that way about my students. (I believe most teachers feel that way no matter what level they are teaching.)

They were so important, a treasure that had to be held in a special way. I treated each of my students according to what I felt they needed for the time being in helping them develop and learn the most they could. I could become close to one and be kind and gentle; try to help that individual make it through some issue while, I am being tough with another one. If you are looking from the outside you would think I favored the one I was nice to and didn't care about the one I was tough on. Not true.

Well, if I was tough on one it was probably because, he was street wise, and / or was spoiled by the parents where he/she didn't think they had to do anything to earn credit in school. So, I was giving them structure and responsibility. Whereas the one I was nice to probably, had been abused and had emotional issues that understanding something was a bit difficult. So, I was trying to give the student some self-esteem.

Confusion for who they are and what they are is common. They are confused because the educational system is confused. Each year they were labeled something else. One year they were level 1, the next year they were LD, the following year they were L1 and L2. It became a joke for us teachers. Besides the labels, each year the numbers of students allowed in a self-contained classroom would also change. One year it was 18, the following year it was 12, a year later it was 15. They also yearly would change if they students with the same disability would be in all placed in the same classroom, and the then a few years later, they were all separated into multiple disability classrooms; then again into same disability rooms. It was a crazy period in special education. We the teachers felt we were being lead nowhere, and the federal educational system didn't know what they were doing.

During that time in history, there were shows like "welcome Back Kotter", which tried to poke fun at the special needs students. However, they didn't know or realize they were more realistic than the general public knew. In our Special Education self-contained classes, we had all those characters, Vinnie Barbarino, the cute sped with no clue, Horshack short annoying/confusing student and Juan Epstein the racially mixed filled with emotional crappy baggage, and the rest. They made our jobs as teachers worth getting up in the mornings. They made us laugh at ourselves and most of all they made us crazier than we were when we first walked in. They were are our students and they were a family in the classroom. Many of us called our students, "our kids".

This book reflects my fond memories as a sped teacher, and the wonderful students I encountered from grades 3 to seniors at the college level. They helped me understand my own limitations as a sped, as one student told me, "Hey, you are who you are, take and live with it. There's nothing else you can do." I told him, "I can try to change". He said, "Than you would not be you". Food for thought as dumb as it may seem. These are recollections of my experiences as a sped teacher, enjoy.

These are memories of fun, fears, and the craziness I experienced with the sped students; including the time I got shot at, threaten by a mother and pampered by the 5%ers a gang of African American JD's. All in all it was great working with those Speds I will always remember them. They actually taught me a lot. It also has Pointers on how to deal with ED Speds. Believe me the tips are helpful.

I have been asked by some of my college students, if my stories are exaggerated, or just fabricated because some seem too outrageous. I have to tell you, I have not exaggerated or made up these stories. I am telling these stories the way I remember them. I have even left out the really bad situations because I didn't want to deal with the painful memories. I have added at the end of each story, a LESSON LEARNED. This is a lesson I learned from the experience I had. I hope you learn from them as well and see the students in a different caring and loving manner if you don't already.

II. Elementary Speds

The lethal Kindergarten Gang

After a number of years as a sped teacher, I developed a great relationship with the Director of Special Education for the school district I worked in. He was an older small framed Jewish man that always had a cigar in his mouth or hand. He reminded me of the actor, writer producer, Mel Brooks. He was funny and knew a great deal as an administrator and was a top expert in the field of Special Education. I looked up to him as a father and a mentor. I don't think many people did, and he would say that some didn't like him. When people would give him a hard time, and accuse him of mischief, he would say he was the only one that can say he is sane because he was tested and found sane by the courts.

His advice to me regarding teaching was basically that I could do anything to help the students learn, as long as I didn't get myself and him arrested. Anyway, we developed a great relationship, where was use to play jokes on some principals. He started to use me as the trigger shooter. Every year I was sent to a school that was having problems in the 10 schools of the district. I was sent in to investigate and report back to him. Sometimes I would be placed in the classroom to interact with the students and the teachers. Since at times I would find the teachers at fault for the incidents and therefore, when the teachers and principals learned that I was in their building they were neither happy nor cooperative.

This one year my boss called me into his office and told me about an ongoing issue with a kindergarten class and wanted me to check it out and see what I could find out for him. I was sent to an elementary school in the district; where three teachers each had quit their jobs only after a few weeks working with this particular class. The last one was actually sent to the hospital. She was beaten and kicked so much that she was found knotted out on the floor next to the blackboard. It was a kindergarten class of 8 Speds students. All 5 to 6 years of age. All three teachers claimed it was the kindergarten students.

I arrived on a Tuesday and was provided the room number in the front office. They were expecting me. I had a reputation of the trouble shooter. I walked the classroom. When I arrived at the room, I stood outside just watching the students and the substitute they had. The children were so small, such babies. How could they have hurt those teachers and placed one in the hospital hmmm. It didn't make any sense.

After a while they noticed I was there and started to look towards the door. I noticed one little African America tiny girl, no taller than my waist and about 30 pounds, was telling the other students that I was there. She seemed to be the leader. I told myself I had to watch her very closely. I decided to walk into the classroom and introduce myself to the class and the substitute. There was the substitute that as soon as I introduced myself said she was leaving. She got her things and walked out. She didn't even say goodbye to the children. I found that odd.

I noted that in my head and I turned to the children and introduced myself and told them we were going to talk. There was a rug in the center of the classroom and I asked the children to all come and sit on the rug. They all looked at the little African American girl and she made a face that they only understood. They didn't move. They just stayed in their seats.

I was right she was their leader. Strange how can such a baby be a leader in such a negative way. She was at the most 5 years old. I figured I had to get her alone. I noticed the teachers' paraprofessional did nothing. She just sat there playing around with her nails. I told her to take the class out for recess and I would stay with the little girl. She said I couldn't tell her what to do.

I quickly informed her that I could, and if she had questions I could call the Director of Special Education. She gave me a dirty look and told the class to go for recess with her. The little girl I'll call Alice, stood by the door, she was the last one in the classroom. She turned to me placing her tiny hands on her hips. She didn't look puzzled, or scared. She actually looked as if she was pissed off at me. I told the aide that Alice was going to stay with me.

Not knowing how to talk to such a young child without treating her as a little cute girl. I had to be serious and she had to know it. I told her, "So do you want to tell me what is going on"? She came out as if she was one of my 17 year old Speds and she stood with her tiny little thin legs apart and said, "we put the last teacher in the hospital and we will put you there too." I said, Are you kidding me?" I thought I have to scare her to get anywhere with her. I responded, "As skinny as you are, I will pick you up and hang you by your legs and make you talk; How about that?" (Of cause I wouldn't do, she was adorable, but I needed to bluff her.) Her beautiful eye opened up as did her mouth. "You can't do that, they wouldn't let you". I told "I don't care what they say", I will get the truth out of you one way or the other."

That's when she said, "Okay, okay, do you see that big jar of lollipops?" I said yes. She said "well it's theirs and we can't get any, even if we are good". I told her I promised her if she worked with me and got the children to listen to me and help me get would get to bottom of this problem I would give 2 lollipops at the end of the day. She smiled and said okay. She said the first 2 teachers, just quit on them. However, the third teacher and Ms. Smith (meaning the aide) would take out the lollipops eat them in front of us and not give us any. Remember, these or only 5 year olds. They don't understand life and mean people yet.

She said they all got angry and tried telling the teacher. But the teacher told them they were Mrs. Smith's and she wouldn't help them. During recess they talked about how they wanted to kick the teacher. They all agreed and so when the class got back to the classroom they all sat down on the rug as usual. The teacher went up to the blackboard to start her lesson. She gave her back to the students while writing the lesson they looked at each other and when Alice got up and ran to the teacher, they all followed and as she started to kick the teacher, so did they. She must have screamed but they did stop. She collapsed on the floor while they continued to kick her.

The aid came in and found the children all around the teacher kicking her everywhere on the floor. They kicked head, her face and her body. She called the front office and reported it. What was missing was the why. Mrs. Smith or the teacher didn't tell the whole story. Was it because of lollipops, I didn't think so. There had to be something else to this horrible story.

The aide gone on her break, and the children were back in the classroom. Alice let them know I was okay. (Remember they are all 5 years old, which is what was so incredible) By the end of the day, the Alice was great and so were the rest of the children. So, I went into the big jar and I noticed they all became very quiet staring at me. I took out the 2 lollipops and gave them to Alice. At first she was hesitant to take them, than of cause she did. I thanked her and told her I would return.

12

The aide came back and I left to write up everything, still puzzled. I went back the next day, although they were not expecting me. When I walked in, I looked for Alice and found her sitting in the back alone with her head down. I walked over to her and said hello. She began to scream and say I lied to her. I was bad. I tried understanding what she was talking about. So, I asked the aide. She informed me that when she returned yesterday from her break Alice had 2 of her lollipops and "she knows better than to take my lollipops". I told her no, I gave them to her.

She told me very loudly, that those lollipops were hers and I was not to be giving them out. I told her that she should have not taken them from Alice that she had earned them. The aide argued, that those lollipops were hers. You cannot give them away. I asked Alice was that happening a lot? The little girl cried nodded her head yes. I turned to the aide and told her to go to the Director's office. She said, "why because of my lollipops"? I informed her it was because she had caused the issues. She had no business working with children and that we no longer needed her. She said she would take it to the board and took her things and left. The kids all starred at me and I called the front office and informed them that I needed another aide and to call the Director. I stayed with those children for a week to get the use to a new teacher and a new aide. I also brought them their own jar of lollipops and candy as rewards for good behavior. I heard later that the children were doing great.

Lesson learned: Criminals are taught not born, no matter the age, you mistreat someone you will get the wrath sooner or later from them, even from a 5 year old angel.

PICA

Pica (/ˈpaɪkə/ PY-kə) is an eating disorder that is characterized by an appetite of non-nutritional substances such as ice, chalk, dirt, or sand. In some chronic cases, in children, they will eat pens, pencils, cardboards, etc.

This is a story of a young boy that was in one of my classes in my early teaching years. It was a 3rd grade class and it of cause was a Sped class. That year we had all different types of disabled students together in the classroom. The E.D.(Emotional Disorders) with the L.D.'s (Learning Disabilities) and ADD's. (Attention Deficit Disorder)

He came into the class later on in the school year. He was introduced to the rest of the class and he sat down and started to do the work I gave him. He was a nice boy. However, he had a number of issues. First and foremost he suffered from PICA. A disorder I became familiar with after I met him. He also suffered from Urinary incontinence. An involuntary urination at the moment his name was called. It was distressing problem for the boy. This condition may have been cause by a profound terrifying incident in his life and I can assure you it was.

The first day in class I gave him a pencil and a paper with math problems for him to figure out so I can see where he was at in terms of the level of the math I can place him into a group. I sat him at a desk next to mine.

Well he sat there in front of me. And after working on the math problems for about 10 minutes, I noticed he ripped the paper and ate half of it. I asked him, "What are you doing? Why did you eat that paper?" he just looked at me, then in a quiet voice he said "I am hungry." So, I told him, when you are hunger instead of eating the paper, tell me and get you some food. He smiled and agreed. (I didn't know he had PICA)

I asked him for the half of paper he had left to see if he had done the work and how much of it. He gave me the paper and he had ripped it where he ended. He said he didn't know the rest if the work so he ate it.

I asked him for the pencil since I had not seen it for a bit. Well, he smiled and said he ate it too. I first thought he was kidding and told him, yeah that's funny, where is the pencil. He repeated that he ate it. I looked at him seeing that he was not kidding but that there was a real problem here. So, I dropped it.

I learned quickly what to give him and what not to give him. For instance, you could not give books with cardboard covers, he would eat them. No, pens, and no pencils. So, I started to bring in peanuts in their shells. I found out that was not a good idea either. He would eat the shells and not the peanuts. So, I started to bring in peanuts with no shells and I would place a few peanuts and raisins on his desk and he understood if he felt like eating he could eat his peanuts. That went pretty good.

Except for one week he came in and informed me that he was foster child and the family that was going to adapt him took him home and when the saw he was eating the garage in the home, they took him back to the adoption agency. He was destroyed. That day he ate everything he could get his hands on. We went to lunch as usual and I was in the teachers' cafeteria when the principal came in looking for me.

I asked him what was the problem. He told me "You have a problem, you have a student that just ate his Styrofoam tray. So, I responded, "maybe he was still hungry." The principal blow up at me, saying "That is not funny, Ms. Detres, follow me." So I did. The other teachers thought it was funny as well, but he just couldn't get the joke. It was not funny, but knowing him I knew he was still hungry.

We got to his office and he stated he was going to call my boss who had the same sense of humor as I did. The principal got him on the phone and told him what happened with the boy and didn't say what I said, only that I was less supportive then he would have wanted. He asked the director, well what do you think about this? My boss's answer was, "maybe he was still hungry". The principal yelled, "that is why your staff do as they please, because they are like you." and hung up the phone. The student continued to eat everything.

I tried bringing in food and things that I thought would help him, but nothing was helping. One day the nurse called me to the health office and informed me he had was there. I went to him and asked him what was going on and he said he ate something that got him sick. I asked him what did you eat? He told me he had eaten a pen and a pencil. He was crying. I wanted to comfort him and make him laugh, so I told him that was the problem. It was the mixture of the pen and the pencil that does not go together.

I told him if he was set on eating those things that paper and a pencil or a pen and paper go together not a pen and a pencil, he looked at me smiled and agreed never to do that again. I told the nurse and she called the ambulance. I stayed with him until he was taken to the hospital. I understand he was treated and came out okay, but was sent to an institution to be cured of this horrible disorder. I never saw him again.

Lesson Learned: You never know what a child has experienced to make him/her act the way he does. Patience is part of teaching any child.

The Conspiracy at the Third Grade level

My boss always kept me jumping from one building to the next. We had 4 elementary schools. This time I was sent to the east side one; to investigate a third grade sped class. Each teacher sent to the class was robbed and the students would out right refuse to do anything they were told to do. So, I showed up at the building as the other teachers walked in. They looked at me and gave me looks. They were probably thinking who the hell she here to bust. Remember I was the trouble shooter. I have to say, never felt welcomed in any building until it was time for me to leave then the principal would usually ask me to stay and ask my boss to allow me to stay. But my favorite place to teach was the high school. I was just happy returning to the school.

My philosophy was, I was not working as a teacher to make friends, just to help the students, the hell with everyone else. (By the way, I should have been a little bit friendlier. I was wrong.) Anyway, I went to the Eastside Elementary and met with the principal as usual and he informed me that no teacher wants to work with these students. He stated they were thieves and bullies and even threatens the teachers. What is so interesting I thought was that this was a 3rd grade class of 12 Speds. 3Rd. graders how intimidating can they be? I was provided the room number and the list of student names.

I walked into the classroom and they were all playing around and throwing things around. I stood in front of the classroom watching them trying to see who the leader of this group was.

It was clear that it was a skinny Hispanic boy with his sidekick that was another Hispanic boy which was big for his age and very heavy; the kind that would be a bully. I thought so that is the muscle and the skinny one is the brains of the group; If you want to call it that. I then decided to get to the bully first. He seemed needy of acceptance,

They started to look at each other and then, look at the skinny boy and at me. I didn't say a word. I stood there for about 15 minutes just looking. They started to quiet down. The skinny boy, yelled out, "So who are you", a new teacher?" then he laughed and the rest followed with laughter. I just kept quiet. I did however; use a technique that I used with my own kids at home. It was the ugly face. You know, those of you that are mothers, the face that says, "If you don't listen to me, I gave birth to you and I take it away".

They quieted down and went to their seats just staring at my ugly face. The skinny boy, whom I will call Tony, said, "Does the principal know you are here?" "Why are you here?" "Who are you?" They started to feel uncomfortable. This is what I wanted. When they were waiting for my response, I opened my mouth and said "I work for the federal government, (which I did as a consultant so I was not lying). My name is Ms. Detres. I'm here to see if you need my help or if I have to get some of you arrested." Their faces went pale white and their mouths opened up. Tony said, "show us proof" and I just responded "I don't need to show you anything. I know who I am and what I am here for." This set the stage for what I wanted. I informed them I was going to be there with them for a while.

The bully, (That I will call Joey) you know the big kid, well he tried to intimidate me by saying "what if we don't listen to you." I turn and walked to him put my face in front of his, and said, "Whenever they don't listen to me, or cooperate with me you will receive the payment." Joey confronted me and said "you can't do anything to me". This was the moment of put up or leave with nothing; so I quickly grabbed him by the arm (by the way I did not hurt him) and took out of the classroom while the others watched in shock.

Once outside the classroom, I saw how scared he was. I had him against the wall, and told him I would make sure he didn't bully anyone ever again. (I want you to know, I just had to establish my grounds and I needed to gain control of this group that had gotten out of hand. He was frightened and nodded when I bullied him. I felt horrible about it, but I had to do it in order to get to the bottom of what was going on. We walked back into the classroom and everyone was watching him. He looked like he had seen a ghost and sat down quietly. That was the beginning of my relationship with this group.

Tony noticed that Joey's demeanor was different. He was afraid, and he wasn't following Tony's demands. I watched as I went through the class lessons that were left and I made some alterations to fit the needs of the students. I always did that. Surprisingly, they were listening to me.

The next thing I did was two days later I left my bag purposely in my desk and I took the class to lunch. Then I gave the key to Joey to get the wooden pass I left purposely. I wanted to see who would steal from me. Since one of the crimes was stealing from the teachers; when we got back I checked my bag and everything was there. The following day I tried another student, the same outcome. I did this with every student and nothing. I finally sent Tony and sure enough the ten dollars I left in my bag were gone.

I had written my name on the ten dollar bill because I knew they would not check that. I was correct. When we got back to the classroom, while they had their paraprofessional watching them, I checked my bag inside and out and the ten dollars with my name on it was surely missing. I walked into the classroom, and asked every student to stand up and away from their chairs and desk. I didn't say anything I just turned to the para and asked her to contact the police that we were in fact arresting a student. They were all surprised, but Tony became pale as if he was guilty. Before I said anything, he yelled out, "I didn't do anything. I promise, I didn't do anything."

I asked him why would he say anything? He started to become fidgety. So, I asked him to come up to my desk and asked him to empty out his pockets. He was reluctant but he did. He took out some gum, and a ten dollar bill. I asked him to take a step back. As he did he said that "the ten dollars is my mothers, she gave it to me." I looked him and I stated, my ten dollars had my name on it. I asked him if I can look at it. He said sure, but it was his. As I opened it up there was my name Ms. Detres. I informed him I had indeed written my name on the bill and it was now missing and he had it. What did he have to say for himself? He started to try to get out of it. When the principal walked in and asked if I wanted the police. I said yes please take Tony to the office and call his parents. The class was in shock and I turned to them anyone else needs to go? No one said anything. I wrote my report and Tony was taken to the police precinct with his parents. They were not surprised as he had been stealing for some time. I gathered it was due to the fact that they were quite poor. However, there is no excuse to steal.

I stayed the rest of the semester to ensure it didn't happen again. All the students were actually good. They had been placed into different classes. As I found out, putting together some children is like chemicals, and you can develop a lethal combination. It only takes one with the negative attitude and brains and another needing to be important as well as, accepted that is a little big, and you have a team of children you have a potential development of criminals. They will conspire to commit crimes as in this group. By the end of the semester they were normal kids again. At the end of the day, Joey would hug me and say good bye for the day. When I told them it was time for me to leave, they were upset. I had to talk to Joey and help him understand how he was used to help commit crimes and to be a bully. He said he understood, but at his age I just don't know.

I know I never heard of him again as a troublemaker in the system. So I guess he did learn. Tony was never seen in the school district again. At least not while I was there.

Lesson Learned: Some combinations of students are lethal, mixing medicines. Each medicine on its own can be good for you, but mixing some together, can kill you.

Yoga

I was working with a group of Speds on an elementary level and they really weren't troubled students, they were all just very nervous and the state had started to require testing scores to evaluate the students' performance. The school was scared their scores would lower the overall score of the school, so I was brought in. My job was to work with them to see if I can help.

I worked with the students, it was 6th grade learning disabled class. I started with simple test on Fridays. They were just spelling test and they were all so nervous even with going over the words every day of the week. I felt horrible for them. The test was coming up and I felt I had to do something. I thought about how nervous I feel when I have to take a test.

These were children that had cognitive learning disabilities; they didn't need to be stressed out that way. There is something wrong in the system when they believe they can capture the true performance of a student or a teacher through organic state written test. NO CHILD learns the same way, specially the Learning Disabled and no child test the same either. These kids have enough stress and issues to have to be worrying about some test that will not reflect their skills nor their needs. I often wonder has anyone bothered to ask the students what they think about these ridiculous testing demands? Not the young ones, but the older ones that have been able to get around the system.

I am certain they would have a mouth full of what they think of those so call performance tests. Lastly, then I'll stop, those test are the same test given in the east coast as in the west coast and throughout the states. Do we have the same systems, and experiences throughout the United States for the children to be expected to have the same names for things from the south to the north; absolutely not. We don't have the same system nor the same experiences. Example, in the west coast they call the sneakers, tennis shoes, we in the east coast call them sneakers. The hot dogs are called wieners. If I ask a child for the east coast what is a wiener they will say they don't know or a man's penis if the child is older. Do you get what I am saying?

Anyway, getting back to the story, I worked with these students nothing seemed to help them. The day for the practice test, and I came into school with a migraine. Everything bothered me. The light in the classroom was really hurting my head. I was trying to do what I could to ease the pain. I thought of the yoga class. I had to take in college and so I thought it would be great if I turn the lights off and do some Yoga with the class. It would relax them, and help my headache. So, I did. Once on the floor, I had them breathing comfortably. Then I told them in their minds to go where they felt the most comfortable and see themselves there. I added a bright warm sunlight and had them relax and enjoy the warmth of the sun. I did this for 15 minutes. Then it was time for them to go to take the test, which was administered in the cafeteria.

I took them, when the scores came out surprisingly, they did very well; some better than the regular education students. I didn't say anything to anyone, only them. They needed to know how well they did.. So I started every morning we would do to Yoga for 15 minutes and the day and classes would go smoothly. Their scores in test had risen greatly and the behavior was also excellent.

The day came for the test, they were ready. So, I set them up with the lights out and they were relaxing the Yoga. I was at my desk, and all of a sudden, the lights went on and the principal was yelling, "What is going on here?" The students jumped up frighten as he continued to yell the same thing over and over. I explained what we were doing and he objected and said it was a bad practice and not to do it ever again.

I tried explaining what was happening to them and how it was helping me. However, he didn't want to hear it. Sometimes the administration is so far from the direct service, that they forget what works and that the teachers that are in the frontlines working directly with the students' do get great ideas and they should be heard.

Well you guessed it. As soon as we stopped doing it the scores dropped and their nervousness returned. The state test scores were horrible.

Lesson Learned: Sometimes you have to think outside the box, in order to help a student. As my boss use to say to me, "as long as you don't do anything illegal, or get us arrested try it."

III. My short Experiences Teaching in Vermont

The Outhouse

I was in Vermont doing my last two years in college as an under graduate in Speech and Hearing. And so, I was doing my practicum in Speech in elementary education. During my teaching practicum, I was assigned to an elementary school in a small town. I was not aware that small meant in the back woods of Vermont in the 70's. Let me tell you what small is.

I was driving on the main road and I was almost there, when I started to notice the gorgeous picturesque mountain views. These mountains are called the White Mountains. It was so beautiful I looked at them for about 2 minutes as I drove. Then I realized I had passed the town a minute ago. So, I turned my car around and started to head back up. I then started to look at the other side of the road. I remember saying OMG, this is what breath is as I passed the town for the second time. So, I stopped and turned the around again. This time I drove looking out for the school. I pulled up at the country store to ask directions because I didn't see any school, only a few small homes. I walked in to town country store which was a ranch 1 floor set up like a store, sort of like a rectangle no longer than 60 feet. It had the post office in the side, the licensing for marriage, fishing and hunting in another side, the grocery store, and to top it off, the Police Department was at the end of the store. (Talking about utilizing space)

I walked up to the clerk and asked, "How can I get to the school. He looked at as if I was not all there. He said, "It's the building next door to us." I was apparently looking for a building that was a bit larger than a small cape. He then added it's to the right from this store. I smiled and said thank you. I walked out the store and looked to my right. There was a small cape with 2 cars parked in the front and a somewhat larger section to park to the back, this was usual parking for a home. So I walked over and knocked on the door. It still looked like a home for me. A man opened the door and I introduced myself as the new student teacher doing my practicum. He was very welcoming and invited me in.

He introduced himself as the Principal, as he walked me into the small foyer. The foyer was just like a home. It had wallpaper on its walls and photos. The house was divided into a hallway with 2 classrooms; one for grades 1 to 6 the other for grades from 7 to 12. He introduced me to his wife. She was the teacher for the grades 1 to 6 room, and he was not only the principal but also the teacher for grades 8 through 12.

He took me to the cafeteria, which was the basement, and it was only for the 1 to 6 th. Graders. The older kids ate in the classroom and in nice weather, outside. I had a tough morning and I wanted I needed to go to the bathroom. So, I asked him where the bathroom was. He told me go down the hallway and at the end take the door to the left. Oh and don't forget your coat. I nodded. I figured it was probably cold in the back of the house, it was winter. So I put my coat back on and walk towards the back. You can see the door from the front. It was painted bright Red. When I got to the back, which wasn't too far from the front of the house, I turned the knob and opened the door.

There before me was the beautiful snow coming down as the door was opened to the back yard of the house. I stood there looking around and saw a path in the snow to a tiny house. So, I figured I had opened the wrong door. I closed it and looked around to see if there was another door. Nope, there was no other door. I looked to my right and nothing and to my left.

The only doors there were the classroom doors near the front of the hallway. I walked back to the principal/teacher and interrupted the class. I said, "Excuse me but I can't seem to remember where to bathroom door is". He looked at me as if puzzled and I said, "It's the Red door at the end of the hallway to the right." I now had the puzzled look. "Okay, that door leads to the back yard." He said yes, it'll lead you to the outhouse.

I couldn't believe it. A school that didn't have a bathroom! It had an OUTHOUSE! Oh my God, I thought how backwards could this get. Needless to say I changed my mind and, I held it until I got home.

Lesson Learned: always go to the bathroom before going out, you never know if you find yourself with an outhouse to do business.

My color offended the students

I was conducting my speech therapy practicum with a small group (3) of the hearing impaired students at the elementary school in a small town in Vermont. Well, they are mostly all small towns. It was early in the day and I had just started to work, when the principal walked into the room I used for speech and called me outside. I excused myself from the students and I met him in hallway. He introduced himself and I told him I knew he was the principal and asked how I can help him. He said one of his teachers for the 3rd grade was out and was not going to come back the rest of the year. She was out on maternity leave and they were unable to find a teacher. He wanted to know if I could do it for them in between the speech therapy I had to do. He also said he had cleared it with my supervisor.

I told him if it was okay with her, not a problem but I really was not cut out to teach. I was not the "sweet soft spoken woman". I am more like the crude cursing every other word and I was afraid I wouldn't be able to control it. He said he thought I was professional enough to have no problems and he needed my help. So, I reluctantly agreed. (this was the beginning of my teaching career).

I dismissed the students I had in speech and the principal walked me to the classroom. It was a nice room. It was bright, airy and very colorful. I thought to myself wow I don't think I could handle it for too long. Not knowing then that the stimulus was so great, (in so much) that a sped could not handle it. I took the sub-plans and started to work with the students. I had never taught before. This was the first time I was in front of a class and acting like a teacher. While I taught the lesson, the students kept asking me if my hands were dirty. At one point, I asked way are you guys asking me that. Well, a few of the students started to say, your face is clean but your hands are dirty. I told them I washed my hands, why do you say they are dirty? And one student said, they are darker than your face. I realized it was a lack of understanding ethnicities.

Firstly, let me describe this population. The town I was in although I had not seen the parents, but all the students reminded me of the old movie, "The Village of the Dame" because they were all blond and had blue eyes. I on the other hand had red (dyed) hair with a white face and freckles, but my hands had always been darker then my face. I used to ask my mom why and she wasn't able to tell me why. No one ever noticed until these students. I have a white face with tan Hispanic hands. The rest of my body is somewhat pale, like in between both.

Anyway, I figured since I was going to be teaching these kids for a few weeks, I should teach them about ethnicities, and introduce it in the Science class with the blood and what are the differences.

This I felt would give them the understanding that people are all the same no matter the color of their skin. I went to the principal at the end of the day and told him my idea. He thought it would be great so he gave me the okay. The next day, I started the lesson with just my class. By the time the lesson was half way through I had 3 classes. He had told a few of the teachers about my planned lesson, and they snuck into my classroom and they sat in the back of the room listening quietly. I talked about the color of the blood and if we have a vile of an African American blood and a vile of a Caucasian individual would they know the difference? I have to admit it was a great lesson. All the students asked questions and for their ages, they were involved. The principal was in the lesson as well. When it ended the teachers and students clapped.

The principal came up to me and told me, "You are cut out to be a teacher." "You have the skills and attitude to be a teacher". I quickly told him, no I don't want to be a teacher thanks. I have a bad temper and I'm afraid I can hurt someone. He said, "Mirian, you are a born teacher. You had the attention of everyone in the room, including the teachers and me." "There is nothing to think about. I smiled and walked away. Never giving it much though; I was not going to be a teacher. I guess he was right, 35 years later as a teacher and administrator.

Lesson Learned: Not many are colorblind.

Denied a Job Due to My Ethnicity/Color

I sat there in the classroom with the rest of the students. It was a very important day. We were all seniors and had completed our two teaching practicum. We were all excited as we were going to be told our placements as teachers. I was one of three students that received an A+ for both practicums. So, I felt I was one of the first to be placed as a teacher. We were informed that the school district selected the top grades first. So, I was excited as the other students.

The professor came into the class, and we all gave him our undivided attention. He smiled and said a few jokes and then congratulated us of a fine job. He began to call out names and their placements. I was Ramirez then so I figured he was calling the students names alphabetically. He quickly came to the R's and passed it into S's. My name was not called. I thought maybe it was a mistake.

Eventually, he called out all the students and their placements and I was not called. He congratulated everyone again and dismissed the class. I looked at him, and he told me we need to talk. I stayed behind to talk. After the students had left, I walked up to him and asked him why he not called my name since I had an A+ in both practicums.

The professor was always very supportive of me so I felt comfortable with him. I trusted him. He was a hippy looking short white haired and bearded white man. He told me Vermont was not ready for diversity. It was 1976, I would have thought the opposite but after what I had experienced in Vermont I understood.

He told me he tried getting me a placement but no school district was interested. He said I should just go back to New York and he was sure I could get a placement. He even offered a letter of recommendation for me, but I was the only student that he was unable to be placed. He apologized and that was that. I walked out with the confirmation that I was not wanted there. My professor was great Mr. Woods, He helped me a lot a wonderful man. Years later through the internet I wrote to the college and informed them of all the mistreatment I received due to my diverse ethnicity and I receive a large fruit basket. But no apologize. Today, I receive emails from the Vermont College monthly, but it still bothers me and I guess it always will. Lesson Learned: They say Vermont has come a long way. I haven't seen that yet! A fruit basket can't make up for the prejudice I received.

IV. High Schools

The 600 School System

The 600 School is a type of school like an alternative school for behavioral problem kids. At that time it was an all-boys school. It was in the late 70's. Later on those schools became co-ed schools. I guess they found girls that behaved just as badly as the boys. These schools were in a big City. They no longer exist. They were like jails. I personally, didn't like the way the kids were treated. This was before the alternative schools were created. You know each state has their way of handling the behavioral issues in students.

The 600 schools were created for students that had beaten teachers, brought in knives and basically the JV's of the student population. The school was in lock down 24/7. The minute we got in the doors were locked. We had to lock our classroom doors. By the way I was the only female in the entire school.

My first teaching job was in a Southern state. I graduated and move down there. I taught there for 2 years and moved back up North to my home. It was my second teaching job, after the South. I moved up and found out that as a teacher you can always find a job teaching, in those days anyway.

The school looked like a city school. The parking for the teachers was actually the basketball court. I went into the school the first day and was informed that on a monthly basis each teacher had to give 20 dollars to the petty cash. I didn't understand why, but I said okay. A week later I found out. My car battery was stolen. Every week one or two of the teachers would have their batteries, or tires stolen right from the parking lot. I use to say the neighborhood guys were upset at us using the basketball court to park our cars. The male teachers never admitted it. They were all very nice. However, their way of working with the students was a bit different then my way.

Today they are known as Alternative schools for students that have explosive behavior and are uncontrollable. I was the only female teacher and the only female at all in the building. Later on they began to bring in female students, but the year I was there it was just me. I wondered why they picked me to that job. Do I look that tough? Those that know me would say absolutely. But the school administration didn't know me, unless they are psychic.

As impossible as it may seem, I got close to a few of the students. The teachers were okay, but a few were abusive to the boys. The ages of the students were from 14 to 18. These were Juvenile Delinquent's that wouldn't take crap from anyone. But for some reason, they liked me. It wasn't that I was beautiful, actually I'm homely looking, but that was okay, we related. I use to light a sage stick before the students got into the class and they were pretty calm most of the day. You do what you can to succeed with the students. On occasion you'd hear students cursing the teacher's outs and the teachers getting rough with them.

The school had security cops all around. It was kept in lock down 100% of the time. This meant that the teachers would take the students to the classrooms, and locked themselves in the classrooms with the students. This was wrong on many levels but as I stated many times, who hell was I to say anything, I was JUST A TEACHER. I couldn't wear nice clothes to work, even if I had them, I had to wear jeans. In case we had to struggle with the guys on the floor and believe me we did a lot.

There were students that got wild on a daily basis and we the teachers had to get them down on the floor in a safe position so they couldn't hurt themselves or anyone else. It was like a jail. We ate lunch together had gym and academics together. I taught all subjects. Once they were in the classroom, they were not allowed to leave for anything; If they had to go to the bathroom that was a project in itself. After lunch they had to be taken by the security to the bathroom, the entire class at the same time. If one had to go during the classroom, the teacher would unlock the door and call for the security guy to walk them to the bathroom.

The teachers kept the students that were 14 to 18 in the classroom. The special education teachers taught everything. Were we trained to do so? I guess so. We were trained to be teachers. To have the ability to take any subject matter and teach it to the student's. However, we were not taught to control juv's (juvenile Delinquents) I just happen to be good at being tough and able to talk to kids with 75% authority, 25% demanding, and an over layer of a lot of caring. That formula has worked for me for years.

These boys were misdirected, lost their way, very very poor and most of them had never experienced love of a parent. To me they were special. I argued all the time with the bully teachers and I told the boys to tell their guardians, but no one listened to me. One day I even went to the principal and complained about how the boys were being roughed up. His words were, "if you want to stay teaching here", "mind your own business". I told him it was my business, and he told me to get out of his office.

I never went back into his office again. Being the only women in the building I didn't feel too secure. I thought and felt I could trust the boys more than the teachers. Now that is fucked up.

Anyway, that school or type of school does not exist and longer. Thank God for little favors.

LESSON LEARNED: I thought that no student could be harmful, I was wrong. I was almost dead wrong. Never, think you have a student pegged. They can flip on you.

The Suicide Attempt

When I first walked into my classroom in the 600 school system it was scary. It's the first time I admitted being scared but it was my job. The students were all boys that looked at me as if sizing me up. I noticed it and I said, "I'm Ms. Detres, and I am here to teach you and I don't take any crap from anyone. The students were from the age of 14 to 18. A 15 year old named James looked at me very intensely and after 20 to 30 minutes he said, "You're my Mother aren't you"? I told him he was mistaken. I have my 5 kids at home and none of which were him. I told him, "Look at me, we don't look alike." "You are very fair skin, with black straight hair."

He was also short and very heavyset. I was tall and thin with red hair (at the time) and my kids were all tall and thin as well. He stated that I looked like his mother. He described his mother as having red curly hair like me, and was about my height. I asked him when the last time he saw her, he was said he hadn't seen her since he was 5 years old. But he persisted that he knew I was his mother. The weeks and months passed and he continued to persist that I should admit I was his mother.

The class got really tired of him interrupting lessons with his obsession and they would at times tell him off. I had established a great rapport with the class so, they listened to me when I'd tell them to leave James alone. When I defended him, he would say, "you are defending me because you are my mother". I would tell him, "I'm defending you for two reasons, 1. They can kick your butt, and 2. I am your teacher and I will not allow any student to harass or beat on any other student, however, I am not your mother".

The classroom was in the 4ᵗʰ floor. It was an old Gothic structured building. The entire building had gated covering the hug windows. So, there was no threat of anyone falling out or jumping so we thought. One day we came back into the classroom from lunch to find that one of the windows was open and so was the gate. I called down to the office and they said the windows were being cleaned. I didn't think it was great idea to do that during the day when the kids were there, but they didn't listen to me. Remember I'm just a teacher. Anyway we had to go to gym and we did. When we got back as we were walking in Dave(a student that had gotten close to me) told me that James had ran in and got up on the window and was standing on the ledge outside!

I ran over with the rest of the class to find this to be true. I looked out the window and sure enough, there was James standing on the ledge. I looked into the classroom and threw my keys to Dave. I told him to open the door and run to tell the office. Get the Psychologist and nurse here immediately. Dave did as I told him and I turned to James again. James told me, "mom why did you leave me! Why, I miss you so much! I hate it that you left". "I am going to kill myself because of you." I look at him and he was serious. His face told me the pain he was feeling and that he wanted to die. I told him over and over again, "James I didn't leave you. I have the children I gave birth to. If I had you I would still be with you." "You're a great kid; you have so much to live for". But he just didn't listen. He began to argue, and yell. "You had a boyfriend and you loved him more than me didn't you?" I tried to make sense of what he was saying, and I got frustrated. So, I told him, "If you don't get off that dame ledge right now, I promise you I will kill you myself!"

As I turned to check on the class and I took a few steps, I felt someone touch my arm and when I looked back it was James! He had gotten off the ledge and was standing behind me. He said, "You promise to kill me"? As he said that the security ran in with the psychologist, and the nurse. I looked at them and asked the nurse to get me to a shrink this was too weird for me. James was taken out by the nurse and security. We didn't see James for a few weeks, but then he came back to the class with the same issue.

Lesson Learned: Never think you know how they will behave. They will always surprise you.

"I am not Your Mother"!

The student, James continued to question me daily as to where I lived and was I married and did he have any siblings. You know personal questions. I would never give him direct or specific answers, such as "oh, I live far from here". "I have a half a dozen kids". He would hate my responses and refuse to work. I'd tell him, fine, don't work and get a zero. You can stay in the classroom if you don't make any noise if you do, you're out of here, do you understand? He always agreed, he didn't want to go to the office.

The school was tough place for kids. No fooling around. There were teachers assigned at the time out room that would there wait to deal with misbehaved students sent there. It was their duty time in school. These teachers were big and tougher then the boys. To be honest, when I left that school and went into teaching the Speds at regular schools in Long Island, I thought the job was a cream puff job. Comparing it to the boys in the 600 schools, those kids in the 600 school were tough!

Anyway, never under estimate anyone. You never know what they can do under a nuttiness attack stress or illusions. Well I under-estimated James. I thought he was harmless. One morning I walked in to the cafeteria where the teachers had to pick up the students. I did the usual thing. I carried large envelops which had the students names on each one.

Each morning I would pass out large envelopes to each student with their name on it and they would in turn place their "things", in their personal envelop and no questions asked. At the end of the day, I returned the envelopes back to each student for them to take back whatever they had placed in the envelop not to get in trouble. This system was working great until, this morning. As I was saying hello to the students, Dave came up to me and whispered close to my ear, "He has a gun be careful".

I looked Dave, and then quickly looked at James who was sitting at a table near the doors. He was not as his usual self talking and kidding around. He was quiet and had his head down. I turned back to Dave and asked, "James?" yeah said Dave he showed it to me when he came in. He said he was going to get even with his mother."

I told Dave watch him, and I walked over to the security officers that were all around. I informed them about the gum and they told me not to lock my door and to watch him and anything to let them know. (We normally have to lock ourselves in the classrooms with the students. I agreed and continued to talk as if usual. We all always talked and the students would hang out talking to each other or playing games, while waiting for the bell to ring. I began to pass out the envelopes to my students for their things. (Their things were basically joints, drugs. In those days we couldn't search the student's, so I would ask them to put anything that could get them in trouble in the envelops. I didn't want to see or know what they had in their possession.

James never had anything to put in his envelope. This time he took the envelope and kept it for a while. Everyone handed me their envelopes and the bell rang. I told my class, "that's it, let's go." We walked to up the stairs to our perspective rooms. We were in the 4th. Floor and as we walked I thought, what if he does have a gun, what am I going to do? Hmmm.

I had never been faced with a decision like that. I told myself, he just said that, James really doesn't have anything, he is harmless and I let it go. When we arrived at the classroom, the security cop was down the hallway, acting inconspicuous. It wouldn't have mattered; James was the type of special needs student that he wouldn't notice anything. I thought about what the security guy told me, so I unlocked the door and we all walked in. I closed the door behind me but I did not lock it. It proved to be the decision that saved my life. The student's walked to their seats hesitantly. It seemed strange. I think he had told them all what he was planning on doing.

The students acted strangely nervous, as if they were expecting something. I started to collect the rest of envelops' and Dave said, "James put it in the envelop, come on do it". James shook his head no. I listened and after a few of the students' told James "come on put your shit into the envelope", but he refused to place anything in the envelope. He had his right hand in his jacket. He normally wore a regular coat, like everyone else. However, this day I noticed he had on a big leather jacket that seemed to be covering something in his inside pocket. I told him, hey James what are you hiding in there, why don't you put it in the envelope and I'll give it back at the end of the day. For the first time that day, he looked directly at me and said, "No, I have to take care of something." I asked him "what are you talking about"?

That was when I realized Dave was correct. James had a gun and was planning on using it. For some reason, I couldn't get my eyes off of his hidden hand. As I talked to him I had my eyes glued onto his right hand. He then started to talk in an angry voice. "Why did you leave me mom"? "I needed you, I loved you". "Now you show up and say you're not my mother". "Why are you ashamed of me"?

I answered him while I kept watching his hand. By that time, James had taken the gun out in display for all to see. The gun was big with a long a barrow or at least I saw it that way. It was surreal. I felt I was watching a show on T.V. It didn't seem real and it didn't seem as if I would get hurt. He pointed the gun at me. I measured my words closely. As I looked into the barrow of the gun, "James, you know me, if I had given birth to you, I would never have left you". As I said those few words, his index finger began to pull back the trigger of the gun. As soon as I saw the finger move I yelled out, as I was dropping to the ground, "Hit the floor".

Simultaneously as I hit the floor, the black board shattered. He had shot and missed me. I had dropped just in time; the blackboard had taken my bullet. I heard him walking around and as I turned over on the floor, he was standing over me. James was crying while pointing the gun at me again. Then he said, "I won't miss this time". As he pulled the trigger for the second time his hand was hit at that very moment and the shot went the ceiling. The cement ceiling came down on us both. Security had heard the first shot and ran into my classroom. He kicked James's hand and the bullet went up to the ceiling. That security guy saved my life.

As they took James away, he said, "I didn't want to hurt you mom, I just want to be with you". I didn't know what to say, It was the only time I couldn't find words to say something direct to the person. But he was a child that was hurting, I understood. I kept thinking about my children at home. I had just given birth to my baby girl Jennifer. I thought oh my guy, I could have die and she would never have known me. OMG, I then thought about it. That was when I became frightened. I was taken to the principal's office to wait for the police. I was asked to write a report on what happened. I asked the police where they were taking him. And they just said, don't worry, he won't bother or scare you again. I refused to press charges and I told the principal I was taking a few days off because I didn't know if I want to continue teaching.

I wasn't nervous, just perplexed at what had just happened. My instincts helped save my life. I watched his trigger finger, I yelled at the students' to drop down and I dropped drown to the floor. I missed 2 shots. Wow, I felt lucky, and that God really wanted me around. My drive home was a very long 2 hour drive. The drive seemed forever, I just couldn't get home fast enough.

When I got home, I walked into my home and sat down. I looked at all my kids, as I sat there in a daze. My husband looked at me and asked me what happened? "You look like you saw a ghost". I grabbed and hugged and kissed Danny and Jennifer that were my babies. Then I looked at him, and simply said, "I almost died today" "I got shot at twice". As we sat there, my tears started roll down my face as I told him my story. I told him what happened and he became upset and sad.

It was weird, we laughed and we cried together. We laughed at the fact that I had so many kids I would know if I had left one somewhere, and sad at the fact that he thought I had left him and the fact that a mother left a child and he was hurting so much.

Ray said, "Well, you can find another job, you always said you didn't like teaching." "Or you can show them that someone strong loves them". We laughed and I decided I was going to stay teaching. I got back to the school a few days later I heard James had been placed in a mental institute. When I returned, my class treated me with care, for the first week, hehehe.

Lesson Learned: Never think someone is not capable of doing something drastic. Everyone is capable of freaking out.

Cigarette Burn marks

As I had said I got close to a number of the students. One I will name Dan. Dan was 16 years old. He was a pretty smart but a basket case 90% of the time; he always challenged everyone. He cursed with every other word he said. The others would ignore him as they would say things like, He's fucken crazy. I worked on his cursing every day and everyday he challenged me.

He would invite me out to fight on a regular basis. When I would start a lesson, he would curse and carry one before settling in to try to learn and during the lesson he would have explosive episodes. When he had those episodes, security would take him out of the classroom and into a room where the problem students were disciplined. I never knew what they did until I would notice that Dan would come back after a few hours as if he was crying. I would asked him what had happened and he would act as if he was angerier then when he went in, except for not acting out. He would just look very angry but would look down and not look at me. One day he was taken again because he was acting out in the cafeteria.

I had been talking to him about his behavior and he was doing pretty good with his behavior until that day when he came to school angry. I walked over to the discipline room to see what was going on. I heard him yelling and crying, so as a natural mother I thought what is going on with him. I opened the door and he was on the floor. The teacher assigned to that room just said he was acting out. I told them I'm taking him back to the room. They said no he still had a few more minutes to go then they would drop him off. I asked Dan "are you okay"? He nodded and I left.

When he came back to room he was sad. And didn't want to talk or work. He was usually a talkative boy but when he had those episodes, he as silent. A few more months past and the class and I got close. We had good talks. One day we were all talking about socialization and everyone was asked to say something nice about the other person to their right and the bot next to him said, "you are a good basketball player but you sweat a lot, why don't you take you shirt off like the rest of us?" The weather was already warm out and everyone was wearing shorts and tea shirts but Dan came in with long sleeves and long pants. They would play basketball during lunch and while he sweated, he would not take his shirt off. So, I guess the students wondered why he dressed that way and why did he not wear summer clothing. He told the student he couldn't. It was time for them to go lunch, so I walked them down to the cafeteria and went back to my classroom to work my lesson plans.

After 15 minutes of being there someone knock on my door. I looked and it was Dan. I asked him what was the problem, and his response was "nothing", "nothing is wrong, I just want to wear these shirts". I asked him so why did you come up to the room. He said "if I tell you promise you won't tell anyone." I told him no, I can't promise because if something is wrong I need to get help. He looked down and he said, "They won't do anything and then I'll just get hurt more." Here was a boy who was a round 5'10", and as tall as he was something was really frightening him. I told him to come into the class the fan was on because it was very warm out that day and I told him is that the reason why you don't even roll up your sleeves? He said yes. It was as if I was pulling teeth. A guessing game, but it was not a game to this poor boy. He just couldn't get the words out. His tears ran down his face as he stated to talk. He rolled up his sleeves and I sat there in shock and I began to cry with him. His arms were full of little circles. I had to take a closer look and they were cigarette burns! He had 80% of his arms covered in burn marks.

This boy had been burned with cigarettes and cigars. I couldn't talk for a moment, then I said, "these are cigarette burns?" he said, "and cigars". I asked "when did this happen", thinking it was years ago. He said "since I can remember. My aunt is a heroin junky and has been selling me since I was about 4 or 5 for money to men. If you think that's bad, he then said, "If I don't want to do what they ask for, they burn me with the cigarettes and cigars until I give in." "I have the burn marks throughout my body." The entire time as he told me this horrible story he kept crying and choking at times on his tears. I let him talk, and when he stopped, I told him I was so sorry that has happened to him. I promised I was going to do something about it.

Dan said, he tried getting the child protective system to help him when he was a little boy and his aunt told them he was playing around and they didn't follow through with it. He said, "So I know they won't do anything." I couldn't believe it. I told him, I was going to try, and they were going to do something about it. He was already 16 they had to believe him now.

I informed the nurse and she contacted the Child Protective Services. He didn't return to school for a few weeks. I thought maybe something was done. I was happy for him. But one morning he walked in looked me and said, I told you they would do nothing. I was in shock. When we had time, I asked him what happened. He told me they took him out of the home and was placed temporarily in a home and they went to court he spoke and told them everything. She the aunt claimed she was trying to get her life together.

He then said, "So you know what they did, they put her in counseling and gave me back to her!"

I was never as disappointed in the system as I was then. Of cause until later on, I got disappointed so many times that I feel for any kid that falls into the system. We finished the academic year and I quit my job there. I couldn't take the travel but mostly, I couldn't handle the things I was seeing and hearing. When I left, I understood the kids for being so angry. I would be as well if I was going through as much as they had.

LESSON LEARNED: The system doesn't work, Too many children have fallen between the cracks and then we have many angry adults. Knowing me, I would be a pain in the butt trying to help the kids. I guess there are too many kids to keep tabs on. So, I'll try to help just one children or student at a time.

V. A Great Long Island School District

The Barking Student

I was teaching at a high school in Long Island. I had about 18 students that year in the self-contained classroom. I had a great bunch of kids that year. I guess every "year", I felt that way with my students. The class consisted of only ED students. They were tough as usual, the students no other teacher could work with so I got them. It was around thanksgiving and the students already knew me and what they can do and cannot do. During the holidays the kids start to cut out of school early. You know for shopping and partying.

This year was no different. During my lunch period, I was in the teachers café and starting my lunch when one of the security officers came rushing in calling for Ms. Detres (that was my name then). I stood up and said, "I'm Ms. Detres what's up?" the security cop said, "one of your students has freaked out and is cornered at the end of the building, come with me please." He then proceeded to tell me it was a female and they had already called the police department, which gave us about 30 minutes until they arrive. (By the way was across the street from the high school. :)

I asked him what was she doing that they had to call the police department first? He said she was barking and acting as if she was going to bite someone. When we arrived to where she was, I knew who it was from a distance by her red curly short hair. She about my height and thin, but what stood out the most was her freckles and bright red curly hair. She was a funny girl, and didn't stop at nothing if she wanted to do something. She always listened to me and never gave me a hard time, but she was truly an ED. If she trusted you, she was okay. If she didn't trust you, well you were in for it. I'll call her Margret. She was facing the wall making a growling sound, as if she was a dog.

The security stopped me about 10 feet from her and they stood between her and me. I called out to her, "Margret, Margret what's going on?" She turned to look at me and stared for what seemed a long time. I stared back with a smile. I knew this student was harmless but no one else knew that. Then she broke the silence with a loud bark! She barked a few times and turned back facing the wall. I in turn, barked back at her. She looked at me in shock as if saying why are you barking. I started to take small steps towards her while I barked and growled at her, she responding back the same way, with barks and growls. Security kept telling me not to get any closer.

The closer I got, the louder her growls got. I pushed the security to the side and I finally got 2 steps behind her. She turned and stood there looking at me I let out a bark that made her almost jump. Then she said, "Ms.Kole, you're crazier than us, what you're doing?" I told her no, what are you doing? She smiled and said she was cutting out and was caught. She said the security cops were saying they are from the Special Ed classes so she thought she should act crazy since they sounded like they thought she was crazy she figured she would scare them by barking.

I informed her, that her little joke had gotten them to call the police and she was going to be taken away for testing me. She smile and said she'll be back. At that time the police arrived, and arrested her. I told them she was just kidding but they took her to the Mental State Hospital nearby. Within 2 weeks she was back telling the story to the group. It was interesting that since she got back, she became closer to me. As if we had bonded because I spoke her language, barking!

Lesson Learned: Don't play crazy, because you will be taken as such and you can communicate to Speds on all levels and forms as long as you care about them, they will know.

A Father Issue

Special needs students have many complicating issues and most are in emotional pain. The Special Education teacher must be aware of this and treat the students individually according to their needs and issues. This is not taught in college. This is learned through working with this special population. Well, even the psychologist that conducts their assessments should know this; in order to get the best true test results.

I had a student that I will call Ben. He was from another country and spoke with a heavy accent. He was a skinny little boy, with long hair who looked uncared for, or unkept. He was a junior at the high school. His behavior jumped from good to bad depending on the day like most of them. After months of working with him, there was an incident that caused him to open up about his father.

He almost attacked another student who was making a presentation about his fathers and asked the other students questions regarding their fathers. Ben had to be held back he want to jump the student asking the questions.

After I calmed him down I spoke to him, he understood and told the class he was sorry. Then just like that without any encouragement, he said if he ever saw his dad he would kill him. Now I will proceed to tell the story of his father and the fact that he had abandoned the boy and his mom. At the end he blamed his mother which I found strange. Oh, he also said he could not hear the word "father" it made him angry. I told him I understood not a problem. All the students agreed and started to talk bad about their fathers. I had to stop it but it was a revealing conversation.

I felt glad he had taken that step forward. Thought this must have helped him. The following months he worked and was pretty dependable and his up and down behavior had leveled out. One day as I walked into the café to check on "my kids", the new school Psychologist came up to me and asked me to send Ben to his office to be tested. He said it was time for his full assessment. I looked this tiny well-dressed white man and thought he doesn't belong here. This was a school that had 75% minorities that fell under the low-income levels.

I told him to please remember two things, one he has to a difficult time understanding English when questioned because he is from another country and his home language is Spanish not English. And secondly, and most important do not say, question or mention the word father. I explained he has a problem and can attack.

The psychologist told me he knew what he was doing and if he wanted to mention or discuss his father he would. I told him not to be stupid it would set this student bad months or even years, not to. He told me I was only a teacher he was the psychologist. So, I told him well, if Ben jumps you don't come crying to me, I warned you. I turned and walked away.

An hour had not past when the jerk psychologist came running in the front office where I was talking to the Principal. He ran in with his neat white shirt pulled out from his pants, his tie to the side and his hair what he had of it was a mess. It was obvious he had been attacked, hmm, guess why and by whom.

He yelled out Ben the student attacked me. The first thing I asked was where is Ben? But he kept saying he attacked me. I told him you must have said father to him didn't you stupid idiot. You didn't listen to me.

You think you know everything well I just went off on him. He said "yes, I did and then he attacked me." Again I asked where is Bcn? He said the student jumped out the window. Luckily, the school was the school was only two floors and luckily this idiot's office was on the first floor. So, Ben could not have gotten hurt jumping out his window. As I ran to look through the window I told the secretary to get me the student's address and I gave her his full name. I also told the secretary to get the sub teacher to stay with my kids until I get back. I started to run out of the building and the assistant principal started to run after me. He yelled I'm coming with you Mirian. I told him to get his car and as I run off the high school grounds he drove up to me and I get into his car. He had Ben's address.

I told the assistant principal what I had told the school psychologist and his response and now look at what has happened. The assistant principal said he was going to file a complaint against him. That was great, but it wasn't going to help Ben at that point. We drove up to Ben's home. It was pretty close to the school. Maybe a few blocks. We got out of the car and heard nothing. I looked the Asst. Principal and told him if Ben came home it's not going to be good. We knocked on the door a few times and there was no answer. Then we heard a faint weak voice saying, alludame, (which is Help me, Help me) in Spanish. We tried the door and found it to be unlocked. We pushed it open and walked in.

The house was a mess. As if someone had bulldozed the house. It was his mother she was on the floor. I recognize her from when she brought Ben to school the first time. I had a lengthy conversation in Spanish with her and thought she was a nice caring mother. But there she was on the floor and couldn't get up. She seemed in pain she the Asst. Principal ran to her phone and called the police for an ambulance. I asked her about Ben and she said, he had been there and hit her and tore up the house. She said he was furious and talking nonsense. We stayed until the ambulance came. She asked us to contact her family. Once we did, we left the house and went back to the school building which was empty by that time. School was over. It was 4:30pm the time flew and we didn't know where this student was.

The assistant principal told me to go home he would stay around until they found him. The next day I heard they found him in town and he was taken to the mental institution for evaluations. I also heard his mother died later on in the hospital due to a heart attack. The incident was too much for her. I never saw Ben again. I was informed he last it totally when he heard his mother died. He was kept in the mental hospital; all because of the idiot the psychologist.

Lesson Taught; IF someone tells you not to mention something to a Sped, listen and don't. Sometimes, their disability is masking a lot deeper emotional issues that can be harmful.

Bagels and Coffee

It was in the early 80's and there was no known free breakfast in the high school I was teaching in. On a daily basis I had my Speds either out or walking in late. I kept thinking what can be going on? I know that when one came in they would always say, hey Hickey do you have anything to eat? So, I decided to start bringing in bagels and a few cups of coffee for those that drank coffee. Knowing my population the Speds, they all drank coffee but I needed to make sure. That year I had 12 Speds students.

During the day, I started telling those that were in that I was going to start bringing in bagels and cream cheese and for those who drank it, coffee. The first day I came in ½ a dozen bagels, and 3 cups of coffee. I was worried they were not going to come in and the bagels were going to get old. I told myself, I'll try and see what happens.

Well, when the bell rung and the students came into the homeroom period, most of them were there! OMG, I couldn't believe it. I planned a group meeting for the homeroom period. That meant, we took our bagels, and coffee and sat in a circle and we discussed what was pending for the day for them and issues that may come up. It was a connecting group. When I told them this was what we were going to do, there were no objections. I had to spilt the bagels in half and get more cups to spilt the coffee as well.

They did ask if they could ask for the type of bagels they could get. I told them sure they could write it on a paper and it was the beginning of the bagel breakfast and coffee and milk. Every morning I would take the list of the types of bagels to the bagel shop and pick them up. They were fine with it. My plain was successful. They were hungry and came in for the bagel and in the discussions we talked about everything. They disclosed things I felt they would never have if not for the group. They started to even hang out altogether. They actually reminded me of the show Welcome back Kotter. I had all those characters. Once I had the groups going and working well, I started to ask them to place demands on the group. Like, no cutting out after the homeroom period, if they want their bagel they have to attend all their classes. And lastly, what is said in the circle stays in the circle.

You must understand these students were the hard core of the district. They were the ones that one other teacher could not handle and didn't want in their classrooms because they were afraid of getting attacked by them. Most of them were 18 years old, tough and unafraid of lashing out on a teacher, administrator nor other students. These were the emotionally disabled with explosive behavior. After the circle meetings you could not see the anger in them. They became a family and looked out for each other. They never tried to make each other feel bad. The Assistant Principal saw this and one morning asked me, Mirian who pays for those bagels and coffee? I told him, I do, they are my kids, not a problem. He told me, I want to help pay for the bagels. I told him sure, but if he wanted to get breakfast for the entire student body I believed there was a program coming out from the Board of Education that would give the students free breakfast if they were in the low-income bracket.

We found out it was too late for that academic year so he started to pay for half of the bagels and coffee for the students. My Speds started to say good morning to him, and were friendly towards him. Regarding their interactions in school, well they were supportive of each other and didn't get in trouble. It was a great year for them, and one of my better years.

Lesson Taught: you can get more out of honey then vinegar. Everyone needs caring on any level, even the toughest kids.

From stealing cars to hubcaps

Sometimes we believe that many of our students are absent from school because they don't care about school and are just trouble makers. You know there is something wrong when a student who comes in everyday and is so hungry he will eat his bagel and any left overs. I couldn't understand why a particular student was out for about 3 weeks. One day during a circle meeting, he came in and looked the bagels left. Then grabbed one and took a chair and sat with use as if he had been there all along. The others students asked him where he has been, and told me he shouldn't get any bagels for his absence. I told the group it was okay.

I asked him (I'll call him Ed) where was he all this time. He smile put his head down and said he was in the slammer. We all looked at each other since he was a not one of the tough looking kids. He was anything but tough. He was very pale and his hair was so blond that it looked white. He was usually a quite boy. I asked him why he was in the slammer and if he wanted to tell us fine if not that was okay.

He told us his mom was a hooker and a junky and he had 5 younger siblings. He told us he couldn't get a job because he had to take care of his siblings while she would go missing for days. One of the other students asked, "Man, how do you guys eat?" he said he stole cars and pass them on for some money, to feed his siblings. We started to discuss the ramifications of stealing cars, and he being in the slammer. Who would feed those kids when he is away? He said they would not eat at times and they would stay in the house quiet so the social services officers wouldn't take them.

We all talked about this. It was so intense that when the bell rang to go to class, they felt they didn't want to go, they wanted to continue their discussion. They asked me if they could stay to continue the discussion, so I kept them and informed the office of it. I let his peers talk to him and they convinced him if he had to steal, why was he not just stealing food for. Which was true in a criminal self-survival way. He agreed he would not steal cars again. We told him to try doing odd jobs for just a few hours at a time: that way he could take care of his siblings and get some money.

The discussion was finally over and we thought we had helped him. By the way, I do have an earned Masters in Special Education and another one in Human Services Administration and almost completed masters in psychology, so I know a little about what I was doing. But it wasn't my education that helped. It was the fact that I understood them as a sped and a person that came from the ghetto. I knew how it was to go to bed hungry and have a cup of coffee for breakfast at 6 years old. The other students and I believe if he doesn't steal cares he just may not steal anything. Hopefully he listened to our suggestion.

A few weeks passed and things were going well, when he Ed was out again for only one day. When he came in he told us was arrested and let go. We asked if he was stealing food. He said, he was stealing hubcaps because he could get money out of it and his baby sister needed diapers. One of the tough guys said, well at least he is not stealing cars anymore. We all agreed.

He was finally taken in and his siblings they were all placed in foster homes. I don't know whatever happened him.

Lesson taught: You can work on diminishing the crime little by little. Sometimes crimes are committed through necessity and not through greed. Yet, so many of these kids are hungry and alone that they don't have any recourse.

Is Spanish the same as Portuguese?

Well I guess some idiot thought Spanish was the same as Portuguese. Every time my boss called me into his office, I knew it was a different placement due to issues at the school. I learned a lot from him. How to be an administrator and who was important. Which of cause was the students'? I was again called in by the Director of Special Education for the school district. He was a Jewish man that loved the students and his job. He was a king in his time.

We all knew he didn't play around and couldn't be taken advantage of nor fooled. He walked around with a cigar on the side of his mouth and talked though the other side. What a great knowledgeable character. He ran the largest Special Educational department in Long Island. I think we had approximately over 2000 Speds in the school district and that was when special education was starting to grow.

Anyway, he called me in and informed me that a student 12 years of the age had just been transferred to our school district. He did not speak English and when tested he scored 64 IQ and was labeled Educatiably Retarded. The individual with that level of an IQ, is quite limited. He informed me that the boy was having outburst in the classroom they had him in; which was a self-contained special education classroom for the retarded students. (I am using these titles because in those days they were the titles used for the particular students with disabilities). I asked to see his test. It was the WISC and I was surprised that it was in Spanish. I thought, but he is Brazilian, hmmmm. This meant that he was tested in Spanish when he only spoke in Portuguese.

I told the Director, I would meet with the student and see if I can talk to him and retest him but it would have to be in English. I was hoping he had learned enough English to understand me and be able to take the test. The Spanish was out of the question, those scores were definitely wrong.

I met with the student and apparently, he was smart enough to pick up quite a bit of English. By the time I got to test him. I had to struggle with some words and with sign language purse and English I was able to test him in English. His scores were great. Especially with the limitations he had, his FS IQ was 109, no gap in Verbal and Performance of 15 points. They were actually within 5 points of each other; which also depicted no cognitive disability. Now today we cannot use that rationale, but then we could. He was transferred to a regular classroom and did very well. I saw him at the high school a few years later and he was still doing great, planning on going to college. I'm sure he made it.

LESSON LEARNED: DO NOT Test a student in another language other than the one they speak. You will get a false reading in scores.

The Denial due to being special needs students

The high school had the assembly as usual. The high school had 6 Sped classes, and we were not allowed into the auditorium until all the other students were already seated. We were then called at our rooms and told to go ahead to the auditorium. We were seated at the end next to the doors. During the auditorium session, the principal announced that the entire high school would be taking a trip to an event which had to do with drunken driving sponsored by the police department. It was being held at another high school. Everyone was excited and all the students were glad they were going on a trip.

The Speds were not allowed to go on a trip before. During the assembly the regular students were misbehaving and a few had to be taken out of the auditorium. The Speds were fine, no problem. When I heard noise from them I'd give them my look and they would calm down, so no problems. At the end of the assembly, we were always the first to leave. We left with no problems.

In the homeroom, I passed out the permission slips and informed the students they had to have their slips in as soon as possible. We were excited that they were going to be allowed to go on trip. We talked about the behavior and they were talking about how they we going to show the rest of the students that they were better behaved them the rest. I was excited for them. They had improved greatly that past year. It was late April and they were good, funny but well behaved.

The following day they all brought in their slips. I remember taking the slips to the front office and making copies of the slips in case any got lost. I prepared them for the trip prior to the trip. The day of the trip came. The day was so sunny, and bright. It was a great day for a trip we all thought. We were so happy they were all in on time and dressed very neatly. The front office started to announce each classroom and the bus they needed to board. Most of the classes were called except for the Speds. We were in a separate wing of the building (it was not against the law then). We the Sped teachers started to stand outside the classrooms watching and waiting to be called. We noticed some of the buses were already driving away. I told the other teachers, may be they forgot to call us. (Somehow, I knew the principal was pulling one of his crummy actions against us). Another Sped teacher called the front office and reminded them we were all still waiting to go, had they forgotten us. The answer was not what we wanted to hear. The Sped teacher came back to us and stated the secretary informed her that the principal said no Speds were allowed to attend.

What the hell, I was furious and I told my class line up we are going to the buses to attend. They all got up and we walked down the corridor. The walk seemed endless. My thoughts were, he is going to stop me, what am I going to do. However, one thing you must know about many Speds, we may think about the outcomes, and what should our actions be, we never conclude and therefore, we really are spontaneous at our actions, even though we would thinking about the action.

We got to the front of the building where the front office was and the doors to the buses. Sure enough the principal was standing there. I told my students lets show him how well we can behave. As I tried walking towards the doors to get the students on the bus, he stood in front of me and told me to take the class back to my room that they were not allowed to attend.

I asked why, as I waved to the bus driver to wait for us. The principal said, they are going to embarrass the school. I informed him we always act proper in the assembly, so what makes him think they are going to act out. He yelled and tried dismissing me, he said, No, they are not going and told the students go back to your classroom. I yelled at the students and told them, "No you are not going back to the classroom.

You are going on the trip and if the principal stops you guys from attending I will call the newspapers and inform them of how the special needs students were not allowed to attend a school trip". I turned to him and told him "That is not going to look good in the newspapers". He looked at me and said, he would write me up. I told him, "I'll give you the pen". Then I walked into the front office and called my boss. I informed him of what was going on. He always supported my actions and told me to take the students on the trip. I got the students on the bus as the principal went to his office pissed and we went. They behaved better than the regular students. It was a great day. 3 of the regular students got busted for smoking and trying to fight the students from the other school. Yes, it was a good day. When we arrived and were getting off the bus, the principal started to yell at us. "I told you they would embarrass the school". "I told you". I turn to him and told him, "It was the regular students, not the Speds. And we walked away. I was so proud of my kids that day and they were proud of themselves.

Lesson learned: Never under estimate the abilities of the Speds. Sometimes administration know less than the Speds.

The Special Ed Newsletter

I was once again transferred to another school. This time is was a Junior High School. I had been assigned an 8th. Grade class. That is the worse grade level to teach. Let me explain. They are no longer new to the school, like 7th. Graders, when they are intimidated. No, now they feel as if it's home and they are feeling their hormones, like their oaks. They want to be treated like an adult but behavior like little children.

I had to be tough in the beginning of the school year when I felt they could use some self esteem built up, I try to get them involved in school activities. I created a Sped Newsletter. This was around February. They trusted me by than and were comfortable in the school. It was name by the students, "the SPED Newsletter". They were so, excited. I picked the students for particular jobs. Like for reporting the sports of the school district and other school districts, I picked the sports freak to report the schools sports. For dear Abby, it was dear SPED, that job went to Lillian. She was big tough and very opinionated, perfect for her. Those students that couldn't read but could draw, they were assigned the cartoons in the paper. Finally, those students that couldn't draw or writing were assigned to find jokes and had to fit in jokes throughout the newsletter, even games they found.

The best writer, which I have to say wrote better than me was assigned as the news editor and the other students were assigned to write and report on activities around the school district. It was a challenge but they pulled it off. We did however have a problem in the beginning. I hate it when the administrators don't have a clue as to what we are doing and the purpose. This was the case. Our principal had no clue on working with the special populations, the Speds and didn't want to know.

The class got into it. They were gun ho. They spent every minute they had free working on stories, discussing them and writing them. The artist created characters to for the newsletter. They had a blast. It took them a few weeks to put the stories, cartoons, and jokes together. I worked with the artist to create the format and layout of the newsletter. At the end of the work, we understood it was going to be a monthly newsletter and they loved it. Now it all seemed great, however, we are dealing with Speds; we don't do anything in a normal way.

The stories were great such as the sports reports. The difference was they were cruses in the stories. The editor took out the curses and it looked pretty good. The next thing was the spelling and grammar/syntax of the writing. Although, the student's editors were the best writers in the class, they were still way below the rest of the students in the school. We talked about this as a group and we all came to a decision.

The decision was one that I to this day continue to use. The decision came from a student that said, "If you fix everything they are going to think we are the same as they are". "We want them to know and understand what we are going through and how hard it is for us to communicate". I understood and agreed. People tend to think that a learning disability or any disability means that the student is crazy; that is the first thing they think of when they hear disabled then they are treated as such. So, that is why they act out. They believe they are expected to act crazy because they are "are disabled", so they act that way. I fully understand their logic.

So, we corrected the curses and the obvious misspellings as much as we could, but we did not change what they said in their articles. It was great. They felt so interested, so apart of the school, it was amazing. I took the finish original and I went to the office and used the ditto copier and made about 50 copies. (The ditto machine is the machine we used before a copier or printer was invented).

I got the newsletter to the students and during their lunch time they past the copies out. The response was great. The articles were good, the jokes were great and the student body accepted it and more so accepted the students that wrote the newsletter. The Speds were very proud of themselves and happy. The teachers had a problem on why I decided not to make the editing on the grammar and some spelling era's. But after I explained it to them they also understood and thought it was an interesting approach.

However, the principal didn't agree. He called me into his office and said begain with, is there something wrong with me. I said, yeah, but that has never stopped nor hinder me from working and doing my job well. He got angrier. He said, this as he through the newsletter at me is an embarrassment to my school. He went on about how dare I print something without asking him. I interrupted him and told him, I didn't think of asking him, but if I knew he was going to carry on I wouldn't have asked him. Secondly, it wasn't about him, or the school it was about getting students that people and them selves have given up on education and got them to get involved and enjoy it. I informed him, ever since the newsletter started those very students who were absentees all the time, were actually attending school on a regular basis. They wanted to come to school for the first time and were enjoying their assigned responsibilities.

He didn't want to hear it. He picked up the phone and once again called my boss. He told my boss how I had printed up this poorly written newsletter with the students and had passed it out among the students and teachers. My boss told him to send me to his office that he wanted to see me. The principal hung up the phone and told me go to the Special Services Office, your boss wants to see you NOW. He smiled like now you in for it. My boss was on his side.

I said okay, and I walked out his office. I got the permanent sub to take my class. As I drove to my bosses office, I thought I know my boss, he would want the students to get involved even with my newsletter. I arrived quickly as it was only a few blocks away. I walked in and there he was, smoking a cigar talking to another teacher. He looked over and saw me and said, hello Mirian, come in. He asked me to show him what the principal was talking about. I had a copy of the newsletter with me so I gave it to him without saying a word.

He looked at it, read a few things, laughed at the jokes. When he was done he asked me who laid this newsletter out for you? I said I did. I know a little about art from high school so I did it. He smiled at me and said, "This is funny, and great! I love it! You did what others couldn't do. You got these students to get interested and involved. He asked me was I planning on continuing to create a newsletter monthly. I told him yes.

He then suggested, that each newsletter become better in its corrections and written expression. He said you could do this through teaching the English grammar and the use of dictionaries. (No Internet in those days). As you teach them, their writing and their expression would reflect improvement through each newsletter. I thought it was a great idea. So, we agreed on it. I thought he was a genius. He said he would talk to the principal and get him off my back. I went back to the school and dealt with a very angry principal for that year.

The newsletter came out for the next 2 months. Each month I printed 20 to 30 more copies. By the time the academic year was over, I was printing 100 copies. Oh, I had to print them in the Special Services Office; the principal didn't want me using so much paper on it. So, I'd go to the Sped office and got them printed. Then it was over with. School was done and most were graduating to the high school. I know the principal was very happy that they were leaving and even happier when he heard I was leaving as well. I never did Newsletter again.

It was fitting for that particular group.

LESSON LEARNED: If you can allow yourself to think outside the box, you can get any student interested and involved in school.

Destruction Come in Many Ways

There are children that are disabled, that their parents baby them. Because their parents baby them they will act worse then they should. They are just spoiled by their parents. This was the case in this short cut story. A little Red headed female student labeled Learning disabled was always acting out.

She didn't listen to anyone. She would at time kick other students, threw around things like pencils, desks and other student bags when she didn't get what she wanted. Like when she wanted to be the leader in the class line and her teacher would say no, she would throw a tantrum. Scream and cry and throw things.

I was working on another case in the same classroom, and her teacher had resigned. I took the class to try figure out things like usual. I became their teacher and shortly after the redhead darling was starting to act out. You know when you are new to a class the students if young will be scared and act great. After a few days they will start testing you out. As oppose to the older students. They test you right off the bat. There is no honeymoon time.

One morning she came in and a few minutes into the lesson she announced to the class that she had not taken her medication and was going to destroy the classroom. In her words.

I looked at her and responded, "I didn't take my meds and I am bigger and stronger and I can truly destroy everything here." She looked at me with a daring look. She then stuck out her tongue at me. I ran to her and made believe that I was going to take her tongue and ripe it out of her. Drastic yes, but very effective. Not like today, they are so babied that the teacher would be sued or fired. Thank God I don't work with tiny tots any longer and haven't for over a decade.

I got to her and kept telling her to take out her tongue and she kept trying to hide it and then she started to cry "no I did take my meds". I stopped trying to get her tongue, and looked at her and told her. "If you forget to take your meds, just tell me and no destruction do you understand? She was clearly frightened of my madness as she knotted agreeing with what I Said. I felt bad for scaring her, but she behaved after that incident for the rest of the school year.

LESSON LEARNED: That was when I realized that I could tell the real emotionally disabled as opposed to the just spoiled individual. Some spoiled children are so spoiled that the parents even believe they are disabled (instead of thinking or accepting that they were not taught to behave). The parents take them to the doctor and get the doctor to provide medication without any proof of the problem. This is where so many children get their meds that are really making them act worse. They go meds that are for truly disabled children not for the spoil. That is why the behavior continues and even gets worse. Remember, a truly ED student, or a student with explosive behavior cannot control it. They will be disrespectful, misbehave and carry on no matter whom they are with. Those that do not misbehave in front a person that they are threaten by, are NOT ED.

Is She Spoiled or Disabled?

This is just a commentary vary short story of a parent who deserved what she got from her daughter. At the high school I had many types of Speds. Mostly they were genuine. They had disabilities and they were who they were. Trying to make in school. On occasion, I would run into some students that were just spoiled rotten by their parents and were manipulators and self-centered individuals having no disability but their selfishness.

I rather work with disabled students 100% of the time then to work with these self-serving students. Parents have to understand, that although it looks and sounds cute when a 3 year old curses at you, and has tantrum's, or even hits the parent and the parent says oh how cute, (not). If it is not stopped at that age, it will not be cute at a teenager.

With that said, I had a very tough girl in my self-contained classroom. She had from what the mother identified her as Learning Disabled. To my knowledge I would disagree and label her just spoiled. He skills were very good. She could read and write well. Her mathematics were also on grade level. However, I couldn't mainstream her because her mother insisted that she was L.D. and required self-contained. This came from the student because she didn't want to work and so she told the mother that it was the only way she was going to stay in school if she was allowed to stay in the Sped classes. Usually, students didn't want to be in self-contained classes but this was the opposite. She thought she could glide through school and not have to work being in self-contained classes.

So, the mother pushed everyone around to keep her in Special Education, until she came to my classroom. It was the beginning of the academic year. She came into my classroom looking very tough and mean. The boys thought she was very pretty and one of the boys, a cute boy, tall blond and blue eyes was smitten with her. She would make him do everything for her. He was her go for and didn't mind. I stopped her a few times and although she would get upset with me, she never got tough or loud with me. She knew I would not tolerate her negative behavior.

One day in class she just didn't want to work and I told her she had to I would send her to the principals office. She tried arguing so I sent her to the office. I was called shortly after, to inform me that her mother was coming in to talk to me. I agreed and had them keep her in the office.

She stayed there until her mother came in. I was called into the conference room and I met with the mother who informed me that her daughter was allowed to do as she pleased because she was disabled. I thought the mother was a bit off, but I didn't say anything. The student saw her mother and walked into the office where I was meeting with her. She proceeded to curse her mother out. Telling her what the bleep, bleep, bleep, she was doing at the school that she was embarrassing her and she was a bleeping bleep and that she would get her at home when she got there. I grabbed the student and pulled her away from the mother who looked as if she was scared and was being pushed against the wall by her daughter.

I pulled her away for her mother, and got between them. He was now, where against the wall where she had pushed her mother. I blasted her for cursing at her mother and treating her in such a disrespectful manner. The student looked at me and stood quiet. Then out of nowhere, the mother started to curse at me telling me not to treat her daughter in such a way. That she had the right to tell her off because she had come to school without asking the student. I was shocked. I didn't believe this crap. Then again, I got shocked daily with all the crap I heard from the students and their parents.

I turned to her and told her that was why her daughter disrespected her, because she allowed her to do it. I told her I would not be surprised if she would hurt her someday, she had set it up. She looked at me and grabbed her daughter who told her get the fuck off of me. I'm going to class and walked out. I walked out after her and went to my class. The mother tried meeting with me a few times after that, as her daughter got worse to handle. I refused to meet with her. I just told her get a counselor I'm a teacher not a counselor. I recommended that she got a counselor for her self and her daughter. It was a rough year for them. The student came in a few times and was kicked of school for the cursing the other teachers' out and poor attendance.

LESSON LEARNED: You can't always help someone and impose your values on everyone.

AVOID GETTING KILLED

There is something said about the old saying, like "the apples don't fall far from the tree". I had a student that was a tall Hispanic quiet boy. He hardly spoke in English but was in special education. He had a learning disability. He was a bit strange. His mother was very strange. Each morning we took attendance, and sent the absentee list to the front office. There, the secretary would call to the homes of each absent student and question the absence.

I had informed the front office never to call the mother, only send a letter each time the student was out so she knew of his absence. Well, the secretary was out that day and a substitute secretary came in for her. The substitute received all the absentee lists from each teacher. The secretary would contact all the parents of their child's absence. I sent in my absent list to the office with the particular students name included and about 10 minutes later he walked in late to class; But the Sub had already contacted my students mother. When she was informed that he was absent she got very angry and came to school to find out who had marked her son absent.

I called the front office and told them not to mail out any letter as the student had come in late. I started the lesson when I received a call from the front office. The secretary informed me that she didn't know what to do and the principal was having a difficult time with a parent who was saying she wanted to kill me and then the principal.

I asked the secretary what was the parent's name. I already had an idea of who the parent could be. The secretary said she didn't know the woman's name, but when I described her, the secretary said, yes it was her. It was actually the mother of the particular student. The one whose apple didn't fall far from the tree? I called the hallway monitor staff to watch my class while I went to the front office.

As I turned in the corridor I could hear the mother saying, where is she I will kill her, for marking my son absence when he has never been absent. She was correct about him never being absent. So, I walked into the front office and walked right up to the lady I simply she Said, "Well, you should have a cup of coffee and then we can discuss how you can kill me". Everyone in the office was shocked and kept silent. She looked at me strangely at first, then said, "okay I'll have a cup of coffee, then we can talk."

I took her the conference room and I gave her a cup of coffee, and we sat down and I explained what had happened and why she was called. Then I asked "well how do you plain on killing me?" She smiled and said, "I will not kill you. Thank you for explaining." She then got up and said she had to go home.

I walked her to the lobby and the front doors of the high school and said good bye. As I passed the front office, the principal was standing by the doors and told me, "you know you get along with those nutty people because you are just as crazy as they are and it works". I smiled and went back to my classroom.

LESSON LEARNED: Use whatever method to defuse an incident. Even agree with the person until they are calm and can reason.

The Pencil Stabbing Incident

I was at the high school and teaching math to my class. We had a split classroom; meaning one room with dividers in the middle to create two classrooms of self-contained Speds. Each side could hold 12 students. I had 16 and she had 12. I was always given the larger amount of students. The next door Sped teacher was always disappearing and leaving her class alone. She was thin, tall and in love. She told me it was the only time her boyfriend had to talk and so, since we didn't have cell phones in those days, she would go to the teachers' cafeteria to call him every day at the same time.

Since we were sharing a room, we could hear all the noise. My class would complain at times, and I would walk into her section with a bunch of teenage students kissing, and fooling around. I would tell them, my class is trying to work. They all knew me and respected me to some point so they would calm down.

When I'd see the teacher, I'd tell her she has to watch her class because I'm teaching and I can't watch both classes. She wasn't too happy about it and really didn't listen. On this day, they were fooling around a lot so, I told my class keeps working as usual, I'll be back. I went to her section and reminded them of my class, when I heard a trouble yell from my class side. I ran back in and found Patrick with his hand up in the air and a pencil through the palm of it. The girl sitting next to him, stood up and she said, Ms. Detres, he was bothering me and I told him to leave me alone, and when I went to hit him with the pencil, he put his hand up and my pencil went through his hand.

I quickly grabbed his hand, he wasn't bleeding, I just held his hand up in the air and I told the class to stay there until I got back. I passed the next classroom and yelled at the teacher to please check out my class because we had an accident and I was taking him to the nurses' office. The girl came along, because she felt guilty. He was laughing like teenager's would do. Everything was always funny to them. At the nurses' office I filled out an incident report. His mom was called in and she took him to the hospital. He was fine. The very next day he came in and his new girlfriend was the girl that stabbed him with the pencil. How do you like that, to be young again.

The principal called me into his office to discipline me for not being in the room and leaving the kids alone. I explained what was going on with the teacher I was sharing the room with. And He called her in. She denied it so I was blamed for leaving my class alone. He never believed me that I was actually watching both rooms. I never spoke to her again. The following year we got separate rooms.

LESSON LEARNED: Don't leave your students for anything! They are your responsibility not anyone else's.

The Smoking Room

You know we the Sped teachers were not at all innocent. This incident is a great example of it. I had a room at the high school next to the Auto shop rooms. It was a great room as it had a storage room attached and I set it up like an office. The other Sped teacher around my room would have the same lunch break and we would go in the storage room to smoke and talk, you relax. It was great. There were three of us; a guy, me and another female Sped.

We all thought the same of our jobs. We loved our kids and were good teachers. We just had that niche for us to gather to smoked and relax. We would share stories and ideas on teaching and discipline. I was basically new only 6 to 9 years' experience, the male teacher had 15 years and the other female had 2 years. So, I was in the middle. The male and I were close friends with my boss. The female was new and didn't know much about teaching special education students but fit right in with us. We taught her the ropes as they say.

That year the school district passed the policy of NO SMOKING on any of the school grounds. If you were caught, you would get a fine of $250.00. We felt we could smoke because we in the storage room and no one would see or smell it. So, we continued to smoke there. One day on our break the three of us were talking and relaxing in the storage/office room when we heard, Mirian, Mirian are you around. We stopped and looked at each other. Hmmmm, it sounded like the principal. I didn't say anything, and then we heard other voices, like Howard's our director of Special Services, and another male voice.

We were smoking, and the room was full of the smoke. I had a vent in that room and I thought it was connected to the auto body shop classroom. So, I told the other two teachers lets blow the smoke through the vent to the auto shop. So, as we did that I responded, "yes, I'm in the storage room, I will be out in a minutes".

I left them in the room venting it and I walked out to find the principal of the high school, the Director of Special Services, the Speech pathologist for the district, and the superintendent of the school district in my classroom.

I smiled and the principal walked up to me and stood within inches of my face. And said, were you smoking in there? I looked at him straight in his face as he was looking at me, and I said, "Sorry but I don't smoke".

Now, Howard my boss and the Speech pathologist knew me and knew I smoked, but they kept quiet. Howard wanted to inform me of the vent, that it was actually connected to the classroom. Therefore, when we were blowing the smoke thinking it was going into the auto shop classroom, it was actually going into my classroom where they were at! So, he told the principal, that smoke coming out of the vent was actually from the auto shop.

The speech teacher said, "Yes, don't you smell the gas fumes? I just don't know how Mirian teaches in this room," as she grabbed the superintendent by an arm and walked him out and Howard told the principal "you have to do something about that gas smell", "my teachers can't work under these conditions" and winked at me as he walked out having the principal follow him.

Of cause he spoke to me later on that day, and I never smoked in there again. I respected him totally. He was my mentor.

LESSON LEARNED: There are many teachers, but few mentors.

The Medal plate in His Head

I was teaching in the Junior High School in that year and I had a student that I will call Edwin. He had a small frame, but that didn't stop him from getting girls. He always had a girl with him. He had a tan complexion that the girls loved. So, he was very popular. Edwin was also very tough and gave guys and the teachers a hard time.

I had him in all my classes, and when I tried to mainstream him into a Social Studies class, he refused. He just cut the class until he received a failing grade and came back to my class. He just felt comfortable in our classroom. He worked and received good grades. I did notice he suffered from daily headaches.

One day, he came in late and said it was due to his headache. I asked if he had taken his meds as I knew he was on medication for the headaches. He said yes, but at times it just didn't help.

He told me he was not feeling well and during the lunch break he told me he wasn't going to eat he was just going home. I told him to go through the process so he doesn't get in trouble.

The process was going to the nurses' office and having the nurse call home to get a parent to pick the sick student. He said okay and I saw him walk to the nurses' office.

10 or 15 minutes later I was in the teachers' cafeteria and we all hear notices like a fight. We ran out and I saw Edwin arguing with a teacher. He was trying to leave and the teacher was telling him he was in trouble and couldn't leave. But the teacher was pushing him against the lockers.

I walked over and told the teacher to let him go, he's not feeling well. The teacher said he was walking out and I caught him. I asked Edwin did the nurse call home him. He said, yes she did but there was no answer. Then he said, was just not feeling good. The teacher said well then, you can't go without a parent. When Edwin tried to walk out again the teacher pushed him into the lockers and his head banged first and then his body. Edwin had blacked out. I yelled and for the nurse and we called the ambulance. I stayed with him waiting for it to arrive. He came to and told me he was okay, because he had a medal plate in his head. I couldn't believe it. While waiting, I asked him how and why he had that plate in his head. He told me his story.

He said when he was born the day his mom brought him home from the hospital all his family was there to greet him and hold him. His uncle, his mother's brother wanted to hold him and had been drinking. He stool by the window and fell backward onto the window. As he fell, Edwin the baby fell out of his arms and out the window. They lived on the 4th. floor of an apartment building. The baby fell, down the 4 floors onto the shrubs.

He was rushed to hospital and had to have surgery on his baby skull. He lived in the hospital for 3 months. When he got better, they sent him home; to be greeted by the same group of family members and his uncle. Who, took the baby and with a repeated performance dropped Edwin again through the same window. I couldn't believe it. He said then they had to place a metal plate in his head. He stayed in the hospital for over 6 months. He said he had suffered from headaches and seizures since he can remember.

When the ambulance arrived, so did his mom who had been called and finally reached. He was taken to the hospital and I drove his mom in my car to take her to the hospital. I decided to ask her about what Edwin had told me. I could believe dropped once out the window but twice I couldn't believe it. When I asked her, she began to cry and said, yes, it was true and she never spoke to her brother again.

She said she felt it was her fault and has never forgiven herself for it. I told her I understand and I said nothing else. He stayed in the hospital and they sued the teacher. I don't know the outcome. I did write a report on what I saw happened. Edwin didn't come back to school that year. I actually, never saw him again.

LESSON LEARNED: Many of these students have a tale to tell and are hurting in side. We have to be sensitive, but not stupid. We can understand, but not ignore or excuse.

The Bicycle Thief

I had been working with the Sped class in the high school and it was close to the December holidays', I felt we had gotten pretty close as a class. I had a Hispanic student that was very small in frame but a very responsible young man when it can to his mom and siblings. He helped support them by doing odd jobs, from what he had said. I was never told what the odd jobs were.

I'll call him Jose.

Jose's mom would call me to talk to me in Spanish whenever she was having issues with him and wanted me to talk to him. Many of the Hispanic parents did. I was considered their counselor since many only spoke Spanish. I didn't mind, I thought anything to help them get their education and become productive in society was my goal for them.

I lived in the neighborhood and one of my sons who was 9 years old at the time was riding his bicycle one weekend to the store. It was only two blocks away. He came back walking very upset and told me his bicycle had been stolen. He said he left it outside the store and it was gone. He was very upset. I was more upset because I would have to buy him another one.

I went to school that following Monday, and told the students of the theft and gave them the description of the bicycle and if they saw it to just let me know. Jose came up to me and asked a number of questions like the time and where exactly where was it stolen from. I thought it was a bit strange, but I thought maybe he just wanted to help and was interested for that reason.

He then told me something I found strange and that was, "you know those stolen bicycles are painted and resold." I looked at him and asked how he knew that. He just smiled and said "everyone knows that." He said he would see what he could do. And he walked away.

I didn't hear anything until a month later. Around 2am I received a call to my home. When I answered, it was Jose's mom. She was crying saying that he had been arrested and she didn't know why. I tried asking her questions to see if I could figure out the reason but I got nothing. I thought maybe she didn't understand when they told her. So I told her I would go there and see what was going on.

The precinct was across the school and about 15 minutes away for my home. So, I got dressed and drove over to the precinct. I knew a few of the officers there and so when I arrived I asked to speak to one of the detectives that I knew. He came out quickly and we sat down to talk after the greetings. I asked him about Jose. He looked it up and informed me he was picked up for theft. He went on to say it was grand theft. We argued as to why arrest a kid that all he does is helping his mom and is a good kid. The detective said he was caught stealing a bicycle. I still argued, for one bicycle you are going to arrest him? How can you sleep at night?

"You got to have more than that". That's when he said, what do you mean? We busted him. I kept arguing that he should be let out to his mom. After all, I said, "He stole 1 bicycle, come on". The detective looked at me confused and said, "Mirian, it wasn't one bicycle, it was 14! And we went to his back yard where he had about twenty but 14 that we were able to identify by reports from the kids in the neighborhood who reported their bicycles stolen."

I was shocked! My mouth dropped open. What a fool I was I was embarrassed. I had been played by a parent and a student. She knew all along what it was about. She was there and saw them taking the bicycles out. The detective said it was an elaborate operation. They had paint, and they would change some of the parts to make the bicycles look different. Jose had a business selling redone bicycles. I couldn't believe it. I apologized to the detective and I left. I was angry at myself for allowing to be manipulated by the mom. When I got home I called her. It was around 5am but I didn't care. I informed her that what she had told me was not the truth and I was taken back at her allowing this business to go on. I blasted her and I asked her never to call me again. I hung up and I was so upset that I decided not to allow parents to call me at home anymore and I didn't ever again.

LESSON LEARNED: Don't believe everything you're told. Don't put yourself out there for a student until you know the whole truth.

The Threat from a gang, the 5%er's

This was a tough high school class and most of the teachers were afraid of them. They were African American guys all taller than 5.11 in height and were all fit. I believe they worked out just to intimidate people. In any case, they were big looking and they frightened most students and teachers. I also think they frightened the principal as well.

Knowing me, they didn't frighten me. I think it was because I'm too slow, fearless, or stupid. I personally think it's the latter. They knew this and they started to work with me. I had a chart on the wall, Ms Detres LAWS: You will be kicked out if you curse, argue, fight, or be late. You will not wear earrings, or must wear lipstick, etc. You get my drift. I ran a tight ship I had to they were tough. They respected me because I wasn't afraid of them. I did have to get rid of two students by the end of the academic year to show them I was not kidding.

One day I got a new student. He was a new member of the gang, and acted very tough. He was younger than most and I could see how they treated him like second class. I was teaching and I asked him a question he responded with a curse, like fuck you bitch. I looked at him and when I we about to tell him to get out the leader Patrick, told him he better apologize, that he was wrong. He reluctantly apologized and Patrick told me to go on not to bother with him. Now in those days we had the Speds the entire day if they couldn't be mainstreamed, and these guys couldn't be mainstreamed. At the end of the day, the students left and as I was packing up I found a note that said, "I will get you bitch". I thought the only ones in my room were my students and the new student had called me bitch. So, I figured out who it was.

I went home thinking about the note and the next day I came in. I figured, If it's that guy I will share the note with the class. I told the class to write a paragraph on what they liked the most and why for a writing period. I figured with the penmanship I could find out who threatened me; although I already knew but I had to be certain. The lesson went on and I collected the writings and the only one that didn't write anything was the new guy. I asked him why didn't he write anything, he didn't respond.

I decided to tell the group that I had received a note and it was not signed but with the writings I could tell who wrote it. They all wanted to know what it said, so I read it. I than told them I was not scared and If the person was so tough, why didn't they put their name were they scared?

He stood up, Patrick jumped up and grabbed him by the neck. I stood there just looking I tried telling Patrick to be cool, but he told everyone, "be cool, he is supposed to be one of us and he has disrespected her, we will take care of him after school." He turned to him, "if you ever do something like that again, you are as good as dead. Than told him to get the hell out of the class.

I spoke with them after he left the room. I told them not to hurt him. No one talked only Patrick. He informed me that it was not acceptable to disrespect a female especially, someone like them. They had accepted me as one of them. After we talked we went on with the lessons and I reported the student to the office. The day ended, the note disappeared from my desk. So, did the new student, he dropped out of school. I didn't see him again. He was a very angry person. I thank Patrick, because I don't think I could have controlled that student. Thank God for Patrick.

Lesson Learned: No matter the age, show respect to receive respect.

The Pregnancy Test

Having the roughest high school special education students that were ED, I thought I would have had a harder time with them. I was wrong. I guess they knew or felt that I was like them. I had 18 Speds in my classroom and no paraprofessionals. They were a part of a gang, I mentioned in one of my previous stories, named the "5 %" They all were African American, 17 to 20 years of age. They of cause were placed in my class because firstly they had to be in school and secondly, no other teacher could control them and finally, because they didn't listen to anyone. They did what they felt like doing.

Now when I began my academic year the first day of my classes, I always informed my student, that although I was beautiful (lies) and sweet, we had 18 students and by Christmas we would have ½ of them because I would ensure them that if and when they gave me a hard time I would kick them out of school without a chance of ever coming back.

After a few had gone, due to this process, they understood I was not kidding. They started to listen and we began to bond. You have to understand. I had my technique and theory in teaching the sped. I learned after teaching a few years, that there was a progression in working successfully with this type of student. In the first few months they would hate me. That was fine with me as long as they did their work. I had to gain their respect first. By November they would see I was telling them the truth so trust was gained. They would then start to like me. By Christmas we would have a bond like a family. We had great times in the classroom, and the bottom line for me was that they stayed out of trouble which they did and that they learned while thinking they were being cool and again they did.

By April they would be asking me to be their teacher next year. Then they would try to threaten me, by saying they would quit school if I wasn't with them the following year. It was always that way. Although their names and faces changed yearly, the behavior and cycle of progression remained the same.

In those days Sped teachers taught every subject to those that were not mainstreamed, So, I taught English, Math, History and Science. The Science level I had, I taught Biology. It was around December and they were u well in the routine. I had been feeling sick for a few weeks and I didn't understand why. I had bought a pregnancy test and I had it in my bag to use that week when I got a chance.

I had arrived at the school that day and I was feeling terrible. I shared the information with another teacher and she said I should take a pregnancy test and get it over with. I thought this would be a great lesson, so I took a sample of my urine in a vile and began the lesson. The science lesson that day was the pregnancies of varies mammals. It was going great and the students were into it. When it came to the humans, I took out the test and the sample urine. I explained it to the class what I was doing. I wanted them to see how it can be tested. They were totally enthralled. We talked about the negatives and the positives, such as false negatives and false positives. I conducted the test in front of the class and when the results were displayed they screamed and jumped around saying congratulations as if it was a part of them.

We had a discussion on family members that were expecting and the signs and experiences that the women felt during their pregnancy. It was one of the best lessons I ever taught and their participation was 100%. I never got any back talk, nor any problems. It was as if I had become their mother, or they became my guardians.

LESSON LEARNED: There is softness in and caring in all youth, even in gangs. You just have to be yourself. Don't be anything other then yourself so you can be accepted. I also learned that students do want and need discipline, and structure. Unfortunately, some parents don't understand this. They think feeding, housing and giving everything a child wants is showing love. They forget that as parents are the first to teach morals, proper behavior, structure and all essence of being human and loving. This includes discipline.

The Pan Cakes

From the day we all found out I was expecting, the 5 % er's took care of me. The leader Patrick assigned each one something to do for me. I never asked them to, but they cared and wanted to show it. Tasks like cleaning my car! I would find my car clean and when I'd ask, Patrick would say, "you can't ride around in a dirty car, you can get sick and the baby." Another task was that every morning three of them brought me pancakes and beacon from the iHOP in town. I was shocked the first few days, than Patrick told me, Ms. Detres, you have to eat and take care of yourself, so we are making sure of that. I always asked them how you guys pay for this. Their answer was always, "don't worry you need to take care of that baby". For thugs, they were the most caring group of guys I ever met.

Since my husband was a Math teacher at the high School as well, during mid-terms one day, I asked my husband to take me to iHOP. We had time before the testing started. So we went. When we sat down, my husband saw an ex-student of his and get up to say hello. He brought him over and he was great, so polite. He was the cook for the iHOP. My husband asked him how he liked working there. He then started to tell my husband that he had worked there for about 3 years and he loved it until this particular year. He said he was thinking of leaving. We asked him why if he loved the job. He told us that every morning a gang of African American guys would come in and threatens him if he didn't give them what they wanted. We asked him what they want from you. He said all they want every day is one order of pancakes, beacon and juice. They threaten to beat him if he didn't and if he said anything. So, he was afraid and gave it to them. I stood there listening to his story and thinking wow, my students bring me pancakes, beacon and juice every day. HMMMMMM.

I told you I'm a Sped. It takes me time to understand things and then it hit me. They were my students. I reminded my husband about my free breakfast every morning. And we were shocked. We told the cook what was going on. My husband offered to pay him for at least a month of orders. But the cook told him, now that he knew it was for me, it was his pleasure and would continue. My husband arranged with him to pay him once a week for the orders. It made us all feel better about it. You know those students the 5 per centers continued to bring me the pancakes, beacon and juice until I was ready to give birth and I had to take a leave of absence. I have never forgotten them. I actually missed them and their jokes and caring. They were truly great students. A few months after I left, they were all suspended and then kicked out of school. A few years later I heard that Patrick the most caring one and the leader had been shot to death. He didn't have a chance. It was a drive by shooting.

Lesson Learned: Once you share of yourself with others, they will be receptive to you.

The Female Target

Sometimes the gangs are not as friendly or caring as the 5%er's. That year the Hispanic population was big in the high school. And the gangs were very visible. Nevertheless, I would still carry on my system of teaching and gain their trust. That year I had 15 Speds. A few girls were Hispanic and really tough. The boys were tough and didn't care who they shot. I had a female Hispanic student that had been out for a few weeks. She was short tanned and had very long curly ash blond hair. She had a mouth on her. When she started to be out I questioned the class. No one knew anything. I started to ask around if anyone knew what had happened to her.

I went out the classroom and started to ask other students that I thought would know her. I was informed that she in fact was hiding out because she had ratted on one of the gangs and she belonged to a different gang. The gang she ratted on was out looking for her and was going to shot her. I pasted out the word that she needed to come to school.

A few days later during the second period she walked in. She smile and said will you help me? I asked her what she wanted me to do. What help did she need. She said that she had an aunt in Brooklyn New York and she needed to get the metro to New York City where she can hide out at her aunts for a while. Said ok, Ill take you to the train and get you on it after school. I figured she would be safe in school. (It was not like today where there shooting in schools has become an everyday occurrence.) Schools were mostly safe.

However, I thought about it and to make lite of the situation I placed inch size sticky circles in bright orange on each of my limbs. I joked about it and made her laugh. But it was very clear that she was scared. That day she went with me everywhere. She did not leave my side at all. During one class, while I was teaching, a gang member walked. A familiar face, and I said, "hi Carlos, what are you doing here, long time no see." He had been one of mine and had graduated maybe 3 years prior.

He smiled and said his greetings and then asked me to give him the girl. I told him if he remembered how I was, I was not going to give anyone anything. He then told me they didn't want to shot me, because they liked me but I had to get out of the way for them to get her.

I pointed to the sticks and told him, I will not get out of the way. So, if you're going to shot, Target the limbs not the torso. He asked if I was kidding. I repeated my wishes and asked him to Inform his buddies of what I said, but I was not handing her in. He said I was crazy and turned to walk out. I told him, I come from the south Bronx, the true ghetto, I am not afraid of getting shot.

I continued with my lesson. She stayed with me. She was afraid. The end of the day came and she had to leave. I asked her if she had money to go to Brooklyn where her aunt lived. She said she did, but was afraid of getting shot trying to get to the train station and waiting for the train. We stayed in my homeroom until every student was gone. Then we went to the front office and I called the train schedule. Found out the time of the next express train to New York City. It was in 10 minutes. We had enough time to get there to catch the train. I told her I would take to the train station and she had to do as I told her so she could get on the train. They weren't going to follow her because it was an express. She was in the clear.

She agreed we would be alone in the building. We walked to the front doors. I told her to stay very close to me while leaving the building and not to looking or stopping if she hears her name called. She agreed and I got my things together, I looked both ways and told her lets go. She walked so close to me that she was actually stepping on the back of my feet. We got to the doors to the outside and I looked. There outside were members of the gang waiting for her. I walked out with her on my side.

I said hello to the ones I knew and pointed to the stickies. They smiled as they shook their heads. We got to my car and I had her stand in front of me between the car and me while I unlocked my car. I got her into the car quickly and I told her to get on the floor of the car, she did. I got in and started my car. They started to walk across the parking lot towards my car. I hit the gas and took off.

As I drove straight to the train station the train was there and ready to leave. I told her when we get there run closely to me and get on the train. Don't look back and get into the train and hide somewhere. When we arrived at the train station as the train got ready to ready to pull out. We were almost going to miss it. We got out of the car I told her run even f you run faster than me, and she did. We ran staying closely together. She jumped on the train and disappeared. I turned and around and two of the gang cars were pulling up. As I got into my car I told them one pulled up next to me and I told the driver it was a waste to try to drive to New York City with the time of the day. They would not get there before the train. So they should just let her go. He said well, if we see her around in town, we will shoot her. She's safe for now. I got into my car and drove home. I never heard from her again. She was withdrawn from school.

LESSON LEARN: I believe every child is worth saving, even if you lose your self.

In the Scheme of things,
we are not important the children are

With my transfers from building to building on an annual basis, I just couldn't keep my materials, or books. This time was no different. So, this time when I got transferred to the other high school, I took no books, nor materials. So, once I arrived at the building I went to the front office and got my room keys and schedule. Like usual, I was teaching all subjects.

When I arrived at my classroom I was hoping to have books with least a few of the subjects. However the room was barren. Nothing was left for me. No chalk, no paper, no books. Hmm I thought, I will ask the principal. So, I walked to the principal's office and he was there. I introduced myself and he said he was expecting me.

I informed him I was there to setup my classroom. I also told him I was not there regarding a problem, but I was just transfer, which he didn't seem to believe. He didn't seem happy to have me there, oh well. I informed him that I had no books for my classes and I questioned where the storage room was for books. He said they had a storage room but the books were old. I told him I couldn't teach without books and I didn't care at that point if the books were old.

He told me if I could find some books I can take them, but there were no books for my students. Can you image a school district not having books for all the students? Well, that didn't sit well with me. So, I informed him, I will take any books that I find and I walked out of his office. I walked through the corridors of the high school and I saw nothing. All the rooms I tried were locked. I was getting disappointed with the situation when I passed a small room and the door was open.

I stopped and looked in. It had wall to wall book shelves full of books! Wow, I thought I found the storage room of books. I took book off the shelf and they didn't seem old. The books actually seemed fairly new. I checked out another book, and another, and all were pretty much in great condition. So I thought, may be the principal was kidding me about all the books being old.

And there for me to use was a cart. I thought, how convenient. So, I took books for each subject, Science, Math, English, History and Health. I was set. There were boxes of chalk, pencils and pens. I only took one box of each I figured sharing is important. I didn't want to be hugged. I took my treasures to my room and set everything up. I placed the cart back in the room and after setting up my class room I locked up and went home. I took a copy of each book home to write up my lesson plans. I always wrote for 2 weeks ahead just in case things changed and I would have to rewrite them. It was all good. I thought I was set. September came around quick enough and it was time to start teaching again.

I got to school and it was like home, I loved the students, and I quickly got use to my classroom. I thought I may like it here. I hope I would not be pulled out or transferred for at least 2 or 3 years. Everything was going well. Into the first week of school, I was in the teachers' cafeteria and overheard a teacher telling a few of the teachers that someone stole her books! She claimed it was a thief and she was going to press charges. She was very upset. I thought about it. I thought it couldn't be me I took books from the storage room. It didn't look like a classroom. It looked like a storage room. So, I walked out.

A week later, I was teaching the following week and she came to my classroom, she asked if she can talk to me, I said sure. I thought I would take that opportunity to ask her maybe it was her room, hmmm. I walked over to her as she stood by my door. She said she was investigating who stole her books, then said the wrong things. She said, "it was a fkn thief and I'm going to get the person". "Then I am going to tell the entire school about the thief and embarrass them". "Do you know who stole my books?" I looked at her and said, "Maybe the person didn't know the books belong to anyone." She then said, the person must be very stupid. Wait until I get the person. Well, do you know anything? "Thought about it and said, "NOP, I know nothing. After all I just got here."

Another week went by, and she showed up in my classroom again. This time she was really angry and tough. She opened my door while I was teaching and said, "I heard it was you, so give me my books back now." This was in front of the students. I looked at her and responded, "Get the hell out of my classroom. If these were your books, then they are no longer yours! You try to take them, and I will make you sorry you ever said crap to me. I suggest you close the door behind you quietly, before I get pissed off." She looked at me and I guess she saw my ugly face, you know the one us mothers put when we are reprimanding our kids, because she put her head down and walked out quietly and closed the door behind her.

I never heard about her books again. I stayed at that high school for 9 years before I actually moved out of state and left that Special Education department. I have missed my boss Howard, Pete and the students. It was one of the best facilitated school districts I have had the pleasure of working for.

VI. Southern Sped School

Southern Open Classroom Concept

I moved down south the day after I graduated from my undergraduate studies in Vermont. I was lucky I found a teaching job immediately. It was a high school that was built with the "open classroom" concept. May I say whom ever thought of this concept was an idiot and must have never taught students. This concept was bad for all grade levels; Elementary, through high school. The open classroom was basically a gym looking huge room. No wall just chairs facing portable blackboards. The teacher taught 10% of the time because of the noises coming for other classes in the area and students talking to each other from different classes. It was a horrible mess.

Like everything, those that were supportive would say it's just a new concept and when we all get accustom to it, it will work. Well it didn't. It never worked. Sort of like the Obamacare. They push down the population's throat and at the end you will see it just destroys the system more. I have to say, the school system I worked in was the worse I had ever experienced. Not for the faculty but for the students. In those days I don't know if it improved. There were no requirements or responsibilities put on the students. Anyway, the school building had some classrooms for those students that were considered hard to handle. That's where I came in. They separated the students that were disabled. In those days, that was called for. Now it's a lawsuit waiting to happen.

I had one of those classrooms that was separated from the open classroom. There was an adjoining classroom for another ED class. There was a male teacher that the students loved. I would watch him to see what he was doing so I could learn. It was my very first job as a teacher after graduation, so I was hungry for skills. Don't go to the first person you see to learn from you never know what that individual is really doing. As I learned he was not doing the right things.

He would take his class outside daily and the students loved it. Then one day, I came in to work and he was gone. A parent came in also looking for her daughter who was 15. They were both missing. Later on the day, we heard he called in and informed the principal that they were in love and had left the state and they were fine, they just wanted to be together and that was the end of that. I liked the school because my sister worked there in the kitchen and my dad as a custodian. It was great. My sister would give me a milk shake when I got in, and my dad would leave me messages on the board at night. However, the principal approached me one morning and told me teachers were really not supposed to talk to the staff that worked in the kitchen and custodial staff. I asked why, and he said, "We just don't associate with them." I looked at him and I told him, "Well I can't do that because my sister works in the kitchen and my father is one of the custodians." He looked at me with a disgusted look and said, 'well keep it to yourself and do not patronize with them while you are teaching here' and walked away.

That was the end of my job. I was let go a month later. They ask the teacher I had taken over for she was coming back. She was on a maternity leave. I asked about the teaching position the guy left, and I was told they already hired someone for the position. I never told my family about why I was terminated, but suspect it was because of what I told the principal. My dad was then let go as well. My sister who had a different name stayed until she retired a few years later.

Shortly after, the year ended and I was out of a job. They only hired me to cover for a maternity leave teacher who was coming in the following September. I did work as a substitute the rest of the year while I unsuccessfully looked for another teaching job. I moved back to New York after that year.

LESSON LEARNED: I have noticed, that some people get administrators positions and they forget why they got into the field of Special education. They treat everyone students and staff as if they were lower then them. It's sad to have to deal with such self servicing individuals. The purpose of the job is lost, forgotten and the need for extended time off becomes the reason why they got into the field.

VII. Mid-Western State Alternate High School

Alternative Schools Experience

I was going through a nasty divorce and spoke a number of friends in Washington DC, where I was a consultant for grants and programs and I was able to get help to move to a Mid-western state. I bought a home and move with my three youngest kids. Although I was a consultant for the feds, I found a job in a School district. I was a veteran of the Speds so there was no problem finding a job.

The Alternative schools are for students that have behavioral issues and other Emotional Disabilities. I worked in those schools for 2 years and I have to say, I hated it. I use to think New York schools were bad, but these are the worse. I realized New York has a very good educational system. I began to miss N.Y soon after I made my move there. Although, the teachers were more caring and supportive of the students the system itself was none supportive. Anyway, I'm only talking about the teachers I have encountered. The building was similar to a small campus. It had a center court and the building rapped around it. It was an old building in tan color with the Spanish ceramic roof tiles.

We didn't have security guard. This school stood on its own. It ran grades from 9th to high school seniors. As teachers, we were trained in preventive measures, such as defending ourselves because there was no security to do so. We were expected to maintain our rooms locked the entire day, until gym time. This is the time where we took the students outside for a break. Sort of like recess. However, we still had to stay the students. We really didn't have any breaks but a 30 minute lunch break that was always interrupted by an emergency happening somewhere at the school and we all needed to help and rescue the teacher it was happening to.

On the other hand, the regular school districts in this state were structured in discipline and held the students responsible for their actions. There were fines they had to pay for cursing, and fighting. So, it limited the bad behavior of students. The uniforms were also a good idea. There was no exposure in the girl's attire and we did not have to be subjected to seeing the boy's underwear. They had to wear their pants up around their waist like normal. This was a good thing. Going bad to the Alternative Schools the following are just a few stories that I will not forget.

LESSON LEARNED: I missed New York. I realized I was a true New Yorker. I believe the educational system in Long Island and New York City are one of the best in the country.

"Good Morning Whore"!

There was a female student that that was very tough. She was a Hispanic fair skin, muscular body and long dark brown curly hair. She had a mouth worse than a sailor. She was ED and had explosive behavior. She had attacked a teacher in her district high school so she was placed in the alternative school. I'll call her Linda. She didn't get along with any of the teachers. On a daily basis she would threw a fit. Since the classroom doors were locked, she would bang on them to get out. When she was with another teacher and she had a fit, he would open the door and let her out. She'd walk out to the principal's office, cursing all the way.

Every morning I'd see her as I got out of my car in the parking lot and I'd say, good Morning Linda. She would always respond, "good morning whore". I'd smile and keep walking. This day I was not in a good mood. We all have those days that up really don't want to hear crap from anyone. Doesn't matter from who. Well, I got to the school and parked my car. As I walked pas her I once again said, "Good Morning Linda". And she proceeded to say her famous words. "Good morning Whore" but this time I stopped and ran to her stood close to her face and stopped her from finishing her words. I said out loud, "you can call me a bitch, because I am, but never, never call me a whore". "That I am not and never have been". Then I stared at her. She looked back at me and said, you are crazier than me. I said "yes, I am" and I turned and walked into the building.

Believe it or not, that changed her interaction with me for the two years I was there. Every morning I continued to greet her with "Good Morning Linda". And she began to respond, "Good Morning Ms. Bitch". After a few days, she started to respond, "Good Morning Ms. Hickey". And it stayed that way. When she got upset as usual, she would come over to my classroom and ask me if she could stay with me. I would say sure sit down and get some work done.

LESSON LEARNED: There is always good in every person, you just have to see it.

The Attack from the File Cabinet

I was use to dealing with ED students that were not crazy nor did not want to attack anyone in particular me. But this Alternative school had some strange ones. As I said, a true ED student cannot control their explosive behavior. Whereas a spoiled kid that knows how to manipulate the system and their parents can control their behavior when they want to. Those are not disabled but spoiled individuals that are intelligent enough to know how to manipulate situations. Such as the next story I am about to tell you.

This was a male so called ED student. Hispanic short and small body frame which helped me as you will see. From the day he was admitted into the school he would look at me and actually hiss at me. I would try talking to him and he would ignore me and did no classwork. Yet, when I was not near and he thought I was not looking he would carry in conversations with the rest of the class; In particular the female student Linda. Who could put a hurting him if she wanted to.

I found out he was from the same school Linda was from and had a gone out with her, like boyfriend and girlfriend. Well, as time went by he decided he wanted to show that he was just as tough as she. So, he deceived to start bothering me. Not a very smart choice. I would walk by him and he would say nasty comments. I'd try to talk to him but he just didn't want to hear it.

One day I have an IEP meeting to attend for this very student, it was early and I had a break. I decided to go the conference room where the meeting was going to be held and review the paperwork because I knew the meeting was going to be difficult since the mother was 100%

in denial. She felt it was the schools fault and that he was a victim of a poor educational system. That I truly agreed with. But his behavior was totally on him. Being a Sped teacher for years, I knew the difference, it was all him. I also believed he did not have a disability but it was more like he was a spoiled brat. He knew when to turn it on and off. He was cool in front of Linda, and in front of his mother he was like a baby, calling mommy and acting helpless. She ate it up all the time.

So, I walked to the conference room to review and as I walked in I saw a shadow over the file cabinet. It was a 4 draw cabinet so it was a tall one. I didn't know what to expect but being a Sped myself and around Speds for years I know something was happening so as I walked in I turn to the file cabinet and yelled out NO! He freaked out and as he tried to jump on me I stepped back and he fell onto the floor and hurt his ankle. I had been trained, on how to handle attacks by students so I went into the attack mood and called out for help and stood over him but not too close.

The principal came running and the guidance counselor as well. First the principal called out "call the police" then the guidance counselor said "what did you do to him"? He was crying and holding his ankle. He was in his full baby character. I told everyone that came in running, he tried jumping me and I stepped aside and he hurt his ankle. That was the truth. He denied it and was crying out to his mother. He stated I tried hurting him and I always pick on him. The police were called to file a report. Linda the Sped was in the hallway and was hearing him saying those things. One thing about Sped girls I have noticed we are all very honest, to a fault.

She walked up to us, and now there were students all around for the changing of classes. She told him, "You're a liar, you're not the cool guy

I thought you were. You're a wimp". "You told me you were planning on jumping her and sending her to the hospital". "I had told you not to, that she was not like the other teachers. But you still wanted to do it." "You Are fucked you idiot." She started to laugh. His crying stopped and his true personality came out. The one we all knew and actually hated. He cursed her out and as his mother walked in for the meeting she finally heard it with her own ears, him cursing and threatening everyone that he was going to get a gun and "fuck everyone up", as he put it.

Linda looked at me and said, "I couldn't let him fuck with you, I'm the only one that can, right?" I smiled and told her, not even you, but thanks. We smiled and she went to her next class. He was taken out to of the school and I never saw him again. The rest of the year, Linda listened to me, as if she had become protective of me. It was strange.

As the ending of the year approached, my youngest son had become quite ill and he wanted a puppy to keep him company at home, since he had become bedridden. I had mentioned it in conversation and she had heard I guess. I was saying how expensive dogs were. I mentioned he wanted a bulldog. Well, at the end of the school year, she surprised me and brought in a bulldog puppy and told me it was for my son! She said her father breeds them. I told her I couldn't take it and she insisted. I asked the principal and she said why not. After that year, I started to work for the state and never saw Linda again either, but I never forgot the Good mornings she gave me.

LESSON LEARN: Some can be very sneaky. Always be at your guard when working with Emotionally Disabled students.

VIII. Are These Reasonable Accommodation Request Hmmmmmmm

Accommodations??????????

It has been my pleasure of ensuring that the college students receive reasonable accommodations. However, I have received some request that were not even logical or fair. You would think that students after high school would be more mature and realistic. Well, not so my friends. Due to the unrealistic support of the parents, and those guidance counselors at the schools, the student come to our college with unreasonable accommodations expecting unreasonable outcomes.

Guidance counselors at the high schools have allowed the "touchy, feely approach in accommodating students and not providing structure nor allowing the students a realistic experience in preparation to enter the work force and the responsibility of life. They have setup the students with disabilities in such a dependent manner that they have unrealistic expectations from society. From the unrealistic accommodations of the students only requiring to meet 20 to 50% of the curriculum in order for the teacher to have to pass them, because they are disabled, to Allowing the disabled students to walk out of their classes when they feel like doing.

The students have gotten into the bad habit of knowing they don't have to do much work to pass their courses and they don't even have to be in class, they can walk out and say, I felt I had to leave. I have asked students why they are not paying attention to the professors, or why are they getting up and walking out, and the student has informed me that they are disabled and therefore, they can do what they want to. I have told them, that having a disability doesn't mean they are going to pass their courses no matter what they do. A good example, I was called to classroom by a professor who told me that a female student threatened him.

I asked what had happened. He told me that after he gave back the class papers, a student stood up and told him, "You fuck, if you don't change my grade to an A, I will beat the shit out for you." He said he simply asked her in shock why should I give you an A? She told him "because I worked hard on it and therefore, you have to give me the A."

I went to the classroom and the professor was so upset he had stopped the class. I walked in and the student was still cursing at him and threatening him in front of the rest of the students. I asked her to come with me and she did listen to me. However, as she was walking out she turned to him and told him again, that if he doesn't change her grade she would kick his ass.

As we walked together she asked where were we going. She was laughing and acting very tough. I informed her when we get to my office, we would talk about her behavior. I kept quiet throughout the walk. She on the other hand, continued to talk and curse. When we finally arrived at my office, I closed the door and asked her to sit. I then asked where did she thought she was and who did she think she was talking to? To speak in such a disrespectful manner to a professor. She stated she was disabled and therefore, she can do what she wanted because of her disability.

I informed her that her disability which was cognitive Learning disability did not give her right to disrespect and curse at another person especially a professor. She told me, My IEP says if I curse at my teachers, they have to deal with it. I corrected her, by saying, I know what the IEP says, and those are not accommodations. I asked my secretary to bring me her file where her documentation is filed. I wanted to discuss her accommodations and her disability. My secretary brought it up to my office immediately. I read the disability description in her documents, which said she had a Learning Disability.

I informed her nowhere in the description of the disability did it state that she could act strange in cursing the professor out. She said, her guidance Counselor told her she had the right to do what she wanted due to her disability. I told her the Counselor was wrong. She started to argue with me and talking to me as if we were in the street and I was just another person she was cursing out in the street. I informed her in that she could not speak to me in that manner. That we were at a college and explained the environment and her responsibilities as a student if she wanted to remain a student at the college she was going to have to do as I say. I informed her, that as long as she is in this campus, she need's to respect. "Queens' College conduct policies, I will not tolerate disrespect of any kind". If she does it again, I would recommend suspension for a year from the college. She agreed, and said she would respect. She was under the assumption that because she was disabled, she could say and do whatever she wanted, because in high school told her she could. When I asked her who would tell her that she said, the Guidance Counselor at the high school told her if she wanted to express herself she could and the teachers would have to deal with it. After I met with her that day, she changed and we never had a problem with her again.

However, sometimes, there is a negative outcome. I believe it depends on the how the high school Guidance Counselor has trained the student and parents to behave. We've had students that their mothers come along with them to the intakes, and even after I informed them of FERPA (Family Educational Rights and Privacy Act) That does not allow us at the higher education level to speak with the parents unless the student write a waiver giving us the permission to do so. They still went around to the professors telling the professors what to do and what accommodation they require. All not legal or allowable, but they have done it. One mother we even had to get a restraining order to keep her off the campus.

She and her son were caught cheating on a test. While he was taking his test, he was texting his mother the questions he didn't know and she was texting him back the answers. She was spoken to about this and the following test, the son would say he had to go to the bathroom and after a few times doing this, the professor followed him and found him in the telephone booth with his mother looking up in the text book the answers for a few questions. When confronted, the mother simply stated he is handicap and needs my help.

She got him to graduate through cheating on test and papers and lying to professors demanding accommodations and alterations that are not actual real accommodations or alterations for the student's type of disability. She should be ashamed of herself. However, I don't think she is. She got what she wanted. I just think how is this individual going to get a job when he really did not achieve the required knowledge to do the job. I can understand why some professors don't want to provide accommodations, because of the negative experiences they have with these types of people that lie to get ahead.

I know how it works with special services in grades K – 12 with parents being bullies and pushing their weight around to get what they want from the schools. As a parent I understand wanting the best for my children. However, what I may think is the best for my child may not be what is correct for my child. Therefore, when my kids were growing and in school, I left the decision of teaching up to the professionals they know what is the best form to work with each individual child that has disabilities. Being in the educational system for 35+ plus years, I can assure you that not many teachers are there to harm or not educate a student. They are there because they love teaching and want to help the students. Rarely have I found that a teacher that does not like to teach and hates the children. Although there are a few but it's not the common.

The parents love their children, and want the best for them. However, when it comes to a disabled child the trained professional knows best. Some children need to be treated stricter than others. Each child learns differently, through different senses; some learning visually, others auditorially and hands on. They also each have a way of accepting, and absorbing what is taught to them. Therefore, not every child learns the same, as Mrs. Bush claimed with their terrible approach to teaching in the "No Child Left Behind" Which I have to say is crap. Being a special education teacher for over 20 years, I learned at the beginning of my career, that they do not learn the same way and they each require a different time frame for the learning to occur.

It shows how our educational system has deteriorated to such a point where the children's needs are truly not considered but the needs of the parents are; for the administrators to give the parents the power to decide what, how and where their children learn is a lack of responsibility towards the children as well as a horrendous dishonor to the children and to education and not to mention a disrespect to the teachers that took years and spent their money to learn to become experts in the field because they love to teach and work with the children; The parents are not allowing the children to learn and create. They are allowing them to be lazy reflective in our society.

What the hell does the legislators know about education, nothing. They want test results. They believe these results are the answer to educating the children. Why doesn't our country study other countries such as Asia, and how their children are taught. They have some of the smartest children in the world. They are a great example of no nonsense education. The parents have no say in education. The only responsibility the parents have is to send the children to school daily. That is why the educational system is a success. I hope you get my point.

I had a few other situations and strange requests for accommodations. I once saw an IEP that had 75 accommodations during an annual IEP meeting. I laughed and asked who wrote such a list and the parent said she did. I looked at her and asked her did have any educational training and she said no, this is my child, I know what's best. So, I began to read some of the accommodations out loud. One was that her daughter should come in later because she is not a morning person! Another was that she should get an aid, someone to help her. You would think its because she is unable to walk. No, it was to have an aid to go to the house to get the daughter up and dressed for school because she doesn't want to attend school. (Now this was a 5th. grader school student imagine when she reaches high school). She also had that the daughter only needs to achieve 10% of the work In order to pass! And the IEP accommodations were approved by the committee and year prior. I couldn't believe it. Here are just a few of the strangest request for accommodations and some that are not from a student, but staff/faculty.

Pinched Nerve:

A student came in asking for accommodations. She identified herself as a disabled student. When I asked her what her disability is, she said she had a pinched nerve. I asked if she was under treatment and did she have a letter from the doctor identifying it as a disability and the major limitations it causes the student in her life. She said she is not seeing any doctor, but it does affect her memory and so she needs extended time for timing. I asked her to bring in a letter from a doctor identifying her disability and is she being treated for it. She never came back.

A pinched nerve can be considered a disability if it is severe and the person is under treatment. But this was not the case.

Addicted to video games as a disability:

A student walked into my office and asked for help, because as he stated, "I am disabled and I can't do my work because of my disability." I told him to come into my office and asked him to explain his disability. He said he is addicted to video games. I asked him again to explain. So, he said he prefers to play videos then attend school and do any work. I informed him that whether he was disabled or not he had to do the course work if he wants to pass and graduate. He said, but I have an addiction, you have to give me services. I asked what services he is hoping to get.

His response was he was failing his classes and he wanted me to change his failing grades to passing and provide him with extended time for assignments and test so he can have an opportunity to play with his games.

I told him if he actually has an addiction, he needs to be in treatment. Secondly we do not change grades, nor do we give extended time for assignments and test for this type of disability if he does have a disability. He asked me what disability can I use to get extended time? So, I knew he was trying to get over. I told him if he has a disability to please bring me official documentation identifying it and how it limits him.

Carpal Tunnel:

A male student came in for intake saying he is disabled and requires extended time for test and all his assignments. I asked him in and I requested to look at his documentation. That is where the problems began. Firstly, the documentation was 7 years old. Then the documentation stated the individual had carpal Tunnel and was improving with physical therapy. Also the document stated the individual has NO limitations. This is a major piece. The definition of disability itself states that the individual that is disabled must suffer major limitations in one or more areas in their daily life activities. SO, he does not have a disability. I requested him to bring in an updated document identifying him as having a disability and what are his limitations. He said he would so I gave him temp services for one entire semester. He had the use of the Assistive Technology Lab to do his papers. He never came in to bring in his documentation. He failed two classes and wanted me to change his grades because he is disabled. When I reminded him that he had to bring in his documentation, I never heard from him again.

Demands of a Visiting Foreign Student

A young tall and thin good looking man with a tan complexion came into my office stating that he had a disability and was informed in his country if he came to America, as a disabled individual, he could ask for anything and he would be given it. I sat him down and asked him a few questions and tried to find out more information from him as to what he was looking for as services and accommodations. He had no documentation and I informed him he had to bring documentation that identified his disability and I would help him and accommodate him.

I asked him what type of accommodation he felt he needed for his disability. He then shocked me as he said that he "I demanded" an apartment, a bank account and a Car". He then proceeded to say, if I could not give a car, he would accept a "Moped" motorized bicycle.

I informed him that we do not approve those types of accommodations, and I asked where did he get this information that we do? He stated in his country he was informed that if he came to the USA and being a disabled individual, by law the college would have to give the disabled whatever they ask for. I informed him, they were wrong. He argued that I had to or he could sue the college.

I tried informing him on the types of supportive services and accommodations, and he said, no what he wanted and needed was an apartment, a bank account and a car. I asked him if he got anything like that from his country. He said he got a moped. I asked him if he brought it with him to the USA. He said no. I told him maybe if he wants to get around he should send for his moped from his country. He insisted that he would sue us if I didn't give him what he asked for.

I informed him that he can go to a lawyer, but we will not be forced to provide him with those things. He was actually shocked that we don't do that. And upset at the fact that he wasted his time. I instructed him to bring in his documentation for services, and he just stood up and said "no, I will not" and walked out. I stayed in shock for a few weeks. Thinking is that what other countries think we provide the disabled????? hmmmmmm.

Rugs and Camera's

We had a student that had to be on bed rest and therefore, we provided accommodations for him at his home. He received notes for the classes on a daily basis; hewas connected to her classes through the phone, something like a conference call. His test was taken to his home by a proctor who would stay with him until she completed the test and he would come back to the college. This accommodation took $100.00 round trip each time for transportation alone as he lived an hour from the college. The hiring of a staff was another cost. For The student to be a part of the classes she would call in to a specific number and he was connected to the class as in a conference call. There were note takers and a recording of the each class.

He was interested in journalism and wanted to write. So, I spoke to the college newspaper and they were kind enough to accept him as a writer for their paper. He did this from home.

However, this student didn't feel that the accommodations were not enough. He started to demand from our office very expensive accommodations. The first thing he wanted was for us to put rugs throughout all his classrooms so he could hear the lectures clearer. We offered audio-enhancers for the hearing. By the way he did not have a hearing problem. He refused the audio-enhancer. Then requested that we place a camp quarter camera in his classes with a monitor in his home so she cannot only hear but see the classes. This meant hiring staff that were cameramen, and buying cameras in the thousands, they were just not regular cameras. I informed the student we were doing all we could and it was a hardship to the college to purchase all the equipment from our budget, which was less the 100k. Especially when it was his last month at the college because he was graduating that same semester. He became upset and demanded to see our budget to verify what I was saying. I informed him that our budget information was public information and he could view it on the Internet.

I guess he did see it because I didn't hear from him again. However, the very next month in the very same college newspaper I had gotten him into, he had written a very nasty article on me, not giving students accommodations, which of course was all wrong.

The Big Toe

I had a professor that called me and requested for my department to provide him with a handicap parking space. I informed him if he had a disability hangtag he just had to show it and he could get handicap parking throughout the campus. If he didn't then he would be required to bring in documentation from a doctor identifying his disability and would of cause provide him with parking but not handicap parking. He stated, his disability was that he had a "BIG TOE". And that make him disabled and I told him, well if the doctor finds you disabled because you have a big toe, bring me the documentation.

He yelled and carried on that he didn't have to. So, I repeated what accommodation are you looking for. He stated again he needed to park in a handicap spot due to his toe. I tried talking to him and informing him that handicap parking spots are for individuals that have a hangtag issued by the city or the state. If he wanted to park in the handicap parking he needs to obtain the hangtag. I told him that, no one is allowed by law to park in those handicap spots unless they have a hangtag. He was quite upset and refused to comply and blasted me for not caring about his big toe. He began to park in the handicap spots and was given a number of parking tickets until he stopped.

First, the Heavy Doors

I received a call from another professor who complained about the doors getting to heavy for her to open. I asked her if she had arthritis. She said no, but that she was disabled and is requesting accommodations. I informed her of the process and all that she needed was documentation from her doctor identifying her disability and we ensure she would receive accommodations.

I then asked her what accommodations was she looking for. She stated she was wanted a few things. One she wanted her classroom to be moved to the first floor, which I said that is not a problem, I'm sure we can do that go on. She then said she needed to have someone open the doors for her and specially the bathroom doors or to pull the automatic door openers for the bathrooms on that floor.

I informed her that the bathrooms in the first floor and every other floor had the automatic door openers however, if she brought in documentation I could possible accommodate her. She said she needed someone also to push her around in a wheelchair. I asked her why she wanted that. Could she not walk? She said, it was difficult for her to walk too much and therefore, she wanted a wheelchair, and an aide. So, the final list of her request was: a wheelchair, and aide, someone to open the doors for her, to be moved from one floor to the first floor. I told her we can offer accommodations, but an aide was not something that we provided, nor did we provide a wheelchair and an aide to push her around. However, for her to please bring in a doctor's letter identifying her disability and with that we could see what we can provide according to ADA suggested accommodations as per disability. She never came in. I did move her classroom to the first floor.

The Dance Student

I received a call from a professor with a concern about one of his dance students. Most of the professors that call me are truly concern with help a student. This one was no exception. In his discussion with me he displayed his concerns and true desire to help this student. The student was a junior. She had signed into the dance program as her major. This was a concern for this professor as he was the chair and wanted some insight on how does he alter the curriculum to allow her to pass and become a dancer.

His concern was that the student, who is majoring in dance, is in a wheelchair, unable to move below her waist. This was baffling to me as well. For someone unable to walk or move would want to major in dance. Was she unaware that the program entailed 90% of the curriculum work is dancing on the stage.

He stated the dances are done on the stage 70% of the time and the stage is not that big to allow a wheelchair to move around freely and not fall of the stage and his second concern is how is she was going to dance? He stated when the class got up to dance or follow a step she would say she couldn't. He asked her at one point to dance with her arms. But she also refused to. She informed him that she didn't have to dance, and that he had to provide her with an alternative to the dancing. His question was did he actually have to change his curriculum to meet her needs.

My answer was that the curriculum does not change. It had been approved by the state board of Education and therefore, what the professor can do is to alter the methodology of the presentation.

But if it's a dance major degree she was looking for, he cannot change the requirements for her. She is supposed to be able to perform and he or any professor is to treat the student as any other student. She insisted on staying in the major and fought the professor to allow her to do the dance major by writing papers as her performance. He didn't agree. My suggestion was that his presentation be altered and to try to make the dances functional for the student in the wheelchair. This was impossible. However, her obligation as a student is to meet the requirements. Meaning she needs to be able to succeed in meeting the curriculum requirements in order to pass. She eventually dropped out of that program and majored in another.

The Blind Student
Wanted to be a Surgeon

I had a student come to my office to inform me that she wanted to major in pre-med and eventually wanted to go into surgery. She was dead set on this career. She claimed that no one understood that it would be easy for her to become a surgeon. I didn't want to discourage her but I had a few concerns. Firstly she was totally blind and had a dog with her. For the courses she began to take such as the chemistry labs, I had to hire a student that would do the lab for her. She would tell the student what she wanted her to do with the chemicals as she sat near the student informing her what chemicals to use. However, she herself could not see the chemical reaction, while the student aide would do the work.

This worked for classes and labs, but one of the professors called me and asked me how could she become a medical doctor if she couldn't see the patients' cuts, bruises, and rashes? We discussed what she was going to have to do and then was it feasible and legal? She was going to have to hire a person to take all the classes in medicine and anatomy and then if all of that worked, she would have to hire another person to be with her to see her patients. So, was she the medical student and then the doctor? Or was she just going for the ride and the other individual helping her would actually be doing all of the work and earning the degrees and licenses. These were the concerns that came up.

We both agreed and I would have to speak to her. I have found that many individuals with disabilities usually go into the field where their disability is the affected. Such as, the blind individual that wanted to be a medical doctor; then how about the student that could not write at all. It would take her 2 hours to write a sentence, she went into journalism. The mental disorder disabled students go into Psychology and the Dyslexic who went into writing books.

It is normal to want to over come a problem of any type, in particular a disorder that affects you in your everyday life. So, the students will go into that field just to deal with it and to sort of like punching the disability in the face. See, I can understand this.

IX. Terms you may need to know

ED: Emotional Disability: By definition, ED means Emotional and Behavioral Disorders (EBD) This category is broad and the educational systems use to define a spectrum of emotional and behavioral disorders in children. These definitions and their concrete diagnosis are considered debatable due to the behavior depend on a number of factors.

"The 5 models that are used in EBD are: Biophysical, Psychodynamic, Cognitive, and Behavioral."

. (Wikipedia, the free encyclopedia, (2014). Due to the above factors the individual has problems or the inability to learn.

Developmental Disability: A substantial handicap of indefinite duration, with onset before the age of 18 years, such as mental retardation, autism, cerebral palsy, epilepsy, or other neuropathy. (Medical-dictionary. thefreedictionary.com/ **Mobility + impairment, (2014).**

Goals: The annual projections as to where you want each student to reach. I have noticed that individuals that have never written goals and objectives have turned them around and are actually teaching others the wrong meaning of the goals and objectives. The goals are the outcome you are looking for from the work with the student. The objectives are the activities that are done to reach the goals.

IEP: The purpose of the IEP: Individual Educational Plans was used as a plan on providing supportive services for a disabled student. The teachers and administrators write them according to the needs of the individual student. The disability is written up with the annual goals and measurable objectives; along with the accommodations and supportive services to help and address the disability of the student.

MY OPINION: When the parents took them over and started demanding and were given the right to write them and make any changes, according to the "No Child Left Behind" bill, former president Bush created. Since then, Speds are doing what they feel like it and mothers are leading it. You must understand, the mothers are great for loving nurturing and taking care of the home life of a child. When it comes to educating them, I don't care how educated the parents are, they are too close to the element and therefore will not be able to rationally make decisions that will benefit the child. Their decisions will be made according to their feelings and there is where the problem lies. The parents will decide on something that will allow their child to be promoted and or they will make it easier for their child to pass the courses there you have the measurable outcomes.

Once were excellent accountability factors today are used to limit the teacher from really teaching and giving the student a way to do nothing. Today, the % required by a Sped student to pass a course in some school districts is a mere 10 to 20%. And if a student fails the parents blame the teacher. No, they should blame themselves they set it up for their kids to pass without any effort. When I was teaching, the sped students were required to pass 70% of the work. That was feasible and more realistic. This 10 to 20% is a joke. The Sped are not being held responsible and there are two standards. The regular students are required to do all the work and must pass their courses. Yet, the sped is not required to do such thing. As long as they attend class, that's their 10 % and if they write notes that the 20% and they have pass the course even if they are failing every test and paper they get. Is that fair? Think about it. If you tell me they are disabled, well I tell you why do you think they have accommodations?

Special services, Special Education is to address the needs in leveling the playing field for the special needs students so they can perform as the regular students. Not to give them an extra jump, ex-hand over the other students. That then is a double standard. Not fair, not right and definitely not ethical. And the Speds' do not learn anything but how to get around in life manipulating for what they want, instead of working for it. I am disabled, 3 of my kids are as well and none have ever sought out free hands for their disability nether have I. You must work hard everyone should in order to succeed in life.

LD: Learning Disability: When the learning of language and mathematical skills are impeded any of various cognitive, neurological, or psychological disorders are considered in the disability. (Houghton Mifflin (2014)

M.I.: Mobility Impairment: can include any or all of the following:

It is the inability or limitations in moving any or all of the limbs of the body. It can be a deteriorations and control of the bones and muscles and impairment where the individual requires a wheelchair, and or bed rest.

Mainstream: To place a student in a regular classroom when they were academically ready to function on that level.

Objectives: these are the activities/paths that lead you to the projected goals. These activities are measurable. At the end of each academic year, the school can measure how successful the individual was in achieving the goals set by the teacher.

MY OPINION:

These Objectives and goals should be set by a professional NOT a parent. (Don't get me wrong, I have been a parent of 7 kids, and 8 grandchildren and so many years I have in the field, I would not write up nor intend to work with one of my children. Simply because I am too close to them emotionally.) Parents know their child but not have the training and skills to know what activities can help and support the child's disability. As well as the fact that the parent is too emotionally connected to be objective in the structure and discipline needed to for the success of their kid.

The fact that many school districts give the parents the say on how a disabled child is going to be evaluated and taught is outrageous and does not have the child's best interested at hand. They tell the committee what how should be done. They will write up the 504's dictating the activities and worse yet, the percentages of acceptance. Such as a student will achieve 20% of the skills taught in English. This use to be 70 to 80% achievement required for passing. They parents took over and the acceptance percentage dropped to 20 or even 10% acceptance. This is absurd. The child will learn nothing with such limitations. The parent is setting up such limitations, that when the child reaches high school, or college they will not be able to function and the parent will try to do the same through the academic career of the child. Ultimately failing at whatever the individual want to do.

Allow me to explain 20% of the activity. This can be that the child brings in the paper, and the pen, that's 10% of the activity, and listen to the teacher for the lesson, that is the 20%. Or even tried the work but if the child tried and still fails, the child has done the 20% and there for must pass. This is not fair to the child or the rest of the students.

I always tell the parents that are "helicopter" parents, (meaning parents that hover around their child even at the age of 30, 40.) at the college, "If you child graduates from college and seeks a job, are you going to attend the interview for the job?" they look at me and a few have said yes." They will never get a job that way. I also ask them, "What will your child do if something happens to you. They will not be able to function." "Allow them to advocate for themselves." Allow them to grow as individual human beings. Some school districts don't truly don't care about the students only their relationship with the parents to get the support and get what they want.

It reminds me of the "Inclusion" term; it was initially introduced to include step parents in IEP meetings. With the concept "the least restrictive environment per student" the school districts took these terms and created the mess that we have now. They created entirely new use of the term inclusion and least restricted environment. It was created to make the parents happy as well as to allow their districts to use of thousands of dollars which were allocated to special education children to use the money in other areas. But no one will admit it. They took the "least restrictive environment" and decided it meant that every special needs student should be in mainstream regular classes. The school districts then packed the regular classes with 19 out of 25 students are special needs and they place the special education teacher who is specialized in working with these students as an aid. Having regular teachers try to teach these students and the special education teacher running around trying to prove supportive services to multi disabilities in the same classroom. I am talking about trying to keep the ED student's quiet while trying to help the LD understand the lesson and at the same time scribing for those that can't write. I have seen it with my very own eyes and it's absurd and insulting to the profession and especially the teachers that worked hard at getting their degrees and becoming specialized in the field then to be told what to do by an individual who is not what to do. It is not logical. Let the professionals do what they know best how to do the job. It's as if you get on a train and you take over running the train and push the conductor aside the same thing. Think about it.

Psycho-Edu: Are actually, "Psycho-Educational Assessments," conducted to measure the cognitive abilities of a student. This includes 30 sub-mini testing instruments. These tests are usually required every 3 years. They identify their weaknesses in particular areas of their cognitive learning development and the findings can identify the disability if they are Learning Disabled.

About the Author

I am a SPED, raised in the south Bronx. A Sped is a Special Education individual. Although I never received services because Individual with Disabilities Education Act,(IDEA) did not exist I was able to graduate. In those days, we were just called stupid and encouraged to drop out of school. Well I didn't drop out. When I graduated from High School I had a 3.6 reading level and I was proud of it. I went through a lot of changes. I was unable to read so I couldn't find a job. It wasn't easy. I was homeless for a while. However, my priority was my children and therefore, I knew I had to do something for them. It was not easy as I was and still am slow at comprehending many things. My disabilities are acute dyslexic, hard of hearing from one ear and only have approximately 30% of my short term memory.

I decided to attend college. With my persistence and my children as my motivators; I received a Bachelor's degree in Special Education, a Master's degree in Special Education, a second Master's degree in Human Services administration and my pride, a PhD in Special Education. I have been in the field of Special Education for more than 38 years. I have taught students from the age of 3 with Autism to college level courses and have been an administrator for the past 15 + years.

I believe people have the wrong impression of the Speds. Either they pity us too much like many parents and that only leads to intense problems and making the child more dependent on the parents or the child is just considered a trouble maker because he/she can't sit still or read. Out of their frustration they act out. I wanted to talk about the true Sped and the caring and loving individuals they can be.